Seeker

Dian Layton

Original Seeker artwork by Christy Carritt and Chantelle Cook.

DESTINY IMAGE® PUBLISHERS, INC.

P.O. Box 310, Shippensburg, PA 17257-0310

"Speaking to the Purposes of God for This Generation and for the Generations to Come."

This book and all other Destiny Image, Revival Press, MercyPlace, Fresh Bread, Destiny Image Fiction, and Treasure House books are available at Christian bookstores and distributors worldwide.

For a U.S. bookstore nearest you, call 1-800-722-6774.

For information on foreign distributors, call 717-532-3040.

Reach us on the Internet: www.destinyimage.com.

ISBN 10: 0-7684-3162-X
ISBN 13: 978-0-7684-3162-9

For Worldwide Distribution, Printed in the U.S.A.

1 2 3 4 5 6 7 8 9 10 11 / 13 12 11 10

Dedication

This book is dedicated to seekers everywhere.
Walk with the King, and your life be filled with adventures!

Introduction

Hebrews 13:8 says that Jesus is the same yesterday, today, and forever. When He walked on the earth, Jesus told stories. He hasn't changed; He still tells stories. I believe that Jesus has a never-ending supply of stories to tell. Many years ago I was praying about how to teach children about God. I wanted to somehow present to them the exciting, amazing, fun, wonderful Person I had discovered as an adult. I was reading Daniel 11:32 where it says, *"The people that do know their God shall be strong, and do exploits."* I thought about that. The people who *know* their God—not just *believe* in Him—those people will be strong (on the inside), and they will go on adventures! I thought about the children in our church and realized that many of them *believed* in God...but I wondered how many actually *knew* Him. So I prayed, "Lord, please give me some ideas how to accurately express You to children. Please, tell me a story." And right there and then I got the idea of a King and of a group of children who live in the Kingdom of Joy and Peace, but don't really *know* the King... and the adventure began....

Part One

the Adventure Begins

Chapter One

Seeker opened his window and took a deep breath of the fresh morning air. *Perfect!* he thought. *I can't wait to get on the roller coaster again today!*

With both hands cupped under his chin, Seeker dreamily looked out his window. In the distance he could see the flags at the CARNALville of Selfishness waving brightly. Yesterday, like so many other days, Seeker and his friends had spent most of their time at the CARNALville, thinking only about themselves. (Going to a carnival isn't wrong; but going to the CARNALville of Selfishness is *very* wrong.)

The clowns at the CARNALville had introduced a new roller coaster yesterday and encouraged the children to ride it as many times as they wanted; and they had handed out huge free samples of candy. The CARNALville candy was made from the clowns' own special secret recipe. It was so delicious that the more the children ate, the more they wanted to eat. At night, even though their stomachs felt terribly sick, all they could think of was going again the next day to the CARNALville to eat more candy.

Remembering the candy made Seeker's mouth water. He licked his lips and closed his eyes for a long time. Suddenly, Seeker's daydream was interrupted by his mother's voice. "Seeker! It's almost time to leave for the King's Celebration. Are you ready?"

The King's Celebration...oh no! Seeker had forgotten all about the King's Celebration. It was a special day each week of fun and laughter and good food in the Grand Throne Room. The King's minstrels played their instruments and sang new songs for the King. The castle servants served the best meals that anyone had ever tasted; and the Kingdom jesters played games and acted out stories. The jesters made the people laugh so hard that tears rolled down their faces and washed away any sadness that might have been hiding in their hearts.

But there was one very surprising problem about the Celebration. The children didn't like it. The children didn't like it at all. The more time they spent at Selfishness, the more restless they became at the Celebration and the more disrespectful and disobedient they became at home. The only thing that really mattered to the children of the Kingdom was themselves.

Seeker's mother called again, "Are you ready, Seeker?"

Seeker sighed, "Well, I guess I can just forget about the candy and the roller coaster for today."

He reached in the closet for his Celebration clothes and slammed the door.

Seeker's mood was dark and quiet as he walked with his mother, Contentment, and his older sister, Moira, through the village streets. When they reached the Big Rock at the base of the Straight and Narrow Path, Seeker couldn't bear it any longer. He stopped and pleaded with Contentment, "Mom! Do I *have* to go to the King's Celebration?"

Contentment tried to control her surprise. She cleared her throat and said, "Moira, you go on ahead. Your brother and I need to have a little talk." When Moira was well on her way up the path, Contentment turned to her son. "Seeker! You know very well that we go to the King's Celebration every week. We've been going every single week for years—ever since the King brought us out of the Village of Fear into his Kingdom. What's the matter with you?"

"I want to go to the CARNALville today," Seeker whined.

"It seems to me that you have been spending far too much time at that CARNALville lately, Seeker!"

"But Mom! The King's Celebration is *boring!*"

Contentment shook her head sadly. "Oh, Seeker, if only you would get to *know* the King, then you would *love* going to his Celebration." Contentment sighed a deep sigh and turned back toward the Straight and Narrow Path. "Come on."

Seeker and his mother walked up the path. The beautiful white castle with its golden trim sparkled in the sunlight. The Royal Doorkeeper stood waiting at the great front door to welcome the villagers from Peace and Harmony. He smiled at Seeker and Contentment as they entered the castle and walked down the shining hallway toward the King's Grand Throne Room.

At night, Seeker had dreams about that hallway.

He dreamed of taking off his shoes and sliding from one end right down to the other end. Sometimes he dreamed that he and the other children slid together. And sometimes, he even dreamed of being able to explore the castle. He wondered if there were other shining hallways, and he wondered what was inside the castle towers.

Seeker looked up and realized that his mother was far ahead of him, waiting impatiently at the entrance to the Grand Throne Room. As Seeker hurried to catch up, his feet gave just a hint of a slide on the shining hallway floor.

Chapter Two

Three great tables were set and ready for the King's Celebration. As Seeker and Contentment entered the Grand Throne Room and sat down at a banquet table, Seeker waved to his friends. Seeker's friends were very interesting children. HopeSo, KnowSo, and Yes were always confident and outgoing. Giggles, Gladness, and Glee loved to have fun. Dawdle and Slow talked and walked together very slowly. Doodle and Do were always discussing which one of them would get to do something.

The King's acrobats and jugglers ran into the room, performing cartwheels and somersaults across the floor. The Kingdom jesters passed out brightly-colored ribbons and streamers to the villagers, and the Celebration began. The villagers stood to their feet as dozens of minstrels began to make music for the King. Some people clapped, some danced, and some waved the ribbons and streamers. Laughter and music filled the Grand Throne Room and poured out into the world beyond the Kingdom, bringing hope to everyone who would pause and turn their ears to listen.

Then the castle servants brought in golden trays of food that were served to the villagers on glass plates (that wouldn't break if you accidentally dropped one). Delicious smells filled the air. There were platters of roasted meats, vegetables, and fruits of every kind and warm breads fresh from the royal ovens. The dessert trays were set up for everyone to help themselves whenever they wanted—because the Celebration desserts weren't just good to eat, they were also good for eating! Every food at the King's banquet made his people healthy and strong. The villagers stopped dancing for now. They filled their glasses with sparkling water from the Grand Throne Room fountain and sat down at the tables to enjoy the meal. Everyone was happy. Everyone, that is, except for Seeker and his friends. They picked at their food restlessly and thought about the CARNALville.

"This is so boring!" Seeker mumbled to himself. "All you do here is sing, sing, sing! And it's all the King's fault!"

Seeker looked angrily toward the throne, but what he saw there took him completely by surprise. The King, who was usually smiling and friendly, was not smiling. The King, who usually sang along with his people, was not singing. Instead, the great King of Joy and Peace was very, very sad. Seeker had never ever seen such sadness on anyone's face, and the anger he had been feeling inside quickly disappeared. In its place was a deep concern for the King. Seeker was worried.

The music and laughter of the Celebration faded into the background as Seeker watched the King. Why was the King sad? Didn't anyone care? How could the villagers sing so loudly when the King felt like that? Didn't anyone notice that the King wasn't singing with them today? Seeker tugged at his mother. "Mom, look at the King. Why is he so sad?" Contentment looked up from her meal. "Hmmm? I don't know, Seeker; now eat your food."

"But Mom, just look at him! Something is wrong. Why isn't the King singing with us today?"

Contentment put a finger to her lips and whispered, "I don't know why the King is sad, Seeker! Just be content, like me—and enjoy the banquet!" Then Contentment saw the hurt look in Seeker's eyes. "Don't worry, Seeker," she said. "If something is bothering the King, he will take care of it."

Seeker started to nibble at his meal, but he couldn't stop thinking about the King. He looked back toward the throne. It just didn't make sense! There, surrounded by the laughter and singing of his people, the King was sad. Why? Then Seeker realized that the King was looking at the third banquet table. Villagers from Peace and Harmony filled every seat at the other two tables, but the third table was empty. It was filled with food, but no one was there to enjoy it. While Seeker wondered about that, the most amazing thing happened.

Suddenly the King turned, looked right at Seeker, leaned forward, and winked at him!

Seeker's eyes grew big with surprise. He tugged hard at his mother. "Mom! The King! He winked at me!"

"Oh? That's nice, Seeker. Now eat your food."

"But Mom! The King winked at me! He actually winked at me!" A finger to her lips and a glance from his mother made Seeker turn back to his meal. He munched quietly for a few moments. Then, ever so carefully, he turned his eyes again toward the King. A wave of delighted surprise washed over him. The King was still looking right at him! When Seeker's eyes met his, the King leaned forward and winked again.

"Mom! The King! He winked at me *again!*"

"That's *nice,* Seeker. *Eat...your...food.*"

Seeker ate his food, but he kept looking at the King. The King looked at Seeker; Seeker looked at the King; and something began to happen in Seeker's heart.

Chapter Three

That night, as he got ready for bed and Contentment came to say goodnight, Seeker asked, "Mom, will you tell me again what the King did for us? I mean, tell me about where we used to live."

Contentment sat down, remembering. "Fear," she said with a shiver. "We lived in Fear—all the time, every day. It was so awful, Seeker. I'm glad you were just a baby, and you don't remember those days. You don't remember the dragon..."

Seeker sat up. "Oh yeah. Tell me again about the dragon."

Contentment shuddered. "Ugly, horrible, slimy, smelly. He had the most disgusting habit of picking his nose and burping out loud—just to be rude. The dragon used to breathe thoughts into our minds continually—thoughts about being afraid... afraid of everything."

"Afraid of everything?" Seeker echoed.

Contentment nodded sadly. "We were afraid to go outside, but even more afraid to stay inside. We were afraid of people, but more afraid to be alone. We were afraid of the dark, afraid of the light. We were afraid of everything! All the time, every day...we lived in Fear."

Contentment seemed lost in the horrible memories. Seeker gently called to her, "But Mom...Mom...the King changed all that, right?"

Contentment smiled, "Yes, Seeker, the King changed everything! He set us free from Fear. One day, he marched right into the village, looked the dragon right in the eye, and began to sing!"

"Sing?" Seeker echoed in surprise. He didn't remember hearing this part of the story before!

His mother nodded, "That was a strange thing to do to a dragon, don't you think? But it worked! The King sang about not being afraid, about trusting and believing. And as he sang, the dragon became smaller and smaller and smaller, until it disappeared!"

"Wow!" Seeker exclaimed.

"Then the King brought all of us who had lived in Fear into the Village of Peace and Harmony here in his Kingdom." Contentment continued, "And he taught us a song to sing if ever the dragon Fear tried to make us afraid again. It went like this..."

> *Oooky-pooky-spooky fear,*
> *You have no right to come near!*
> *In the King's name, you get out of here;*
> *Fear, be gone, be gone!*
> *Fear, be gone!*

Seeker was impressed. "'In the King's name, you get out of here.' Wow. If you say that, then the dragon Fear goes away?"

His mother nodded, "If you say that, then *every* dragon has to go away. The King's name is like a powerful weapon, and when you use his name against dragons, they know they are in big trouble!"

Contentment put her arm around Seeker's shoulders. "Seeker, I'm so glad we talked about all this. I needed to remember what the King did for us. I've been far too content with life here in Peace and Harmony. I need to be more of a *seeker!*"

Seeker smiled back at his mother. Then he paused and said, "Mom, remember how the King winked at me today at the Celebration? Well, I've been thinking, and well, uh, can I get to know the King, like you do?"

"Oh, yes, Seeker! As long as you *really* want to! That is very, very important. People can live in the Kingdom...they can eat at the King's banquet table every week...but no one actually gets to *know* the King unless they *really* want to."

Contentment pulled back slightly and looked Seeker in the eye. "Do you *really* want to?"

"Uh-huh," Seeker nodded solemnly.

To his amazement, Contentment shook her head and folded her arms firmly. "No. You must *really* want to! Do you *really* want to, Seeker?"

Seeker thought. He thought about his friends. He thought about the CARNALville of Selfishness. He thought about the clowns and the rides and the candy. And then Seeker thought about how the King had looked at him, and suddenly, none of those other things mattered at all. "Yes," he said with confidence. "Yes, I *really* want to!"

"All right!" Contentment smiled as she stood to her feet. "Then you can go tomorrow...to see the King...all by yourself!"

"Tomorrow?" Seeker was surprised. "To see the King? All by myself?"

"Tomorrow. To see the King. All by yourself," Contentment assured him, tucking his blankets around him. "Goodnight, Seeker. Sweet dreams." She put out the lamp and closed the door quietly behind her.

"Wow!" Seeker said to himself, "All by myself to see the King! What am I going to say? What is he going to say? What are we going to say? Hmm...I better practice. Let's see...

"I should be very *official,* stand and say, '*Good day,* Your *Majesty.*'

"Or...maybe I should be more *friendly* and say, '*Hello,* your *Majesty.*'

"Hmm...or maybe..." Seeker's eyes twinkled, "I should have *fun* and say, 'Hey, Your Majesty! What's happenin'?!"

Seeker laughed and then shook his head. "But no, that's not the right way to talk to the King. I'll say, 'Good day, your majesty!' That's the best (yawn). Just think, yesterday all I wanted to do was go to the CARNALville, but now...(yawn) I want to know... the King."

Seeker fell asleep, and he dreamed all night about the King and the castle with the long shining hallways.

Chapter Four

The next morning, when the rooster crowed, Seeker jumped out of bed, got dressed, ran downstairs, ate his breakfast, and headed for the door. His mother was standing there, smiling and holding his toothbrush. "Oops! Forgot about my teeth!" Seeker quickly brushed his teeth and gave his mother a hug. "Bye, Mom! I'm going to see the King!"

"All by yourself," Contentment said with a smile.

Seeker ran through the streets of Peace and Harmony toward the castle. But then, the closer he got to the Straight and Narrow Path, the less confident Seeker began to feel. He slowed down to a walk. "I'm going to see the King," he gulped and walked even more slowly. *"All by myself?"*

He stood at the Big Rock at the base of the hill and looked up at the castle. "Wow. The Straight and Narrow Path never used to look quite so straight and quite so narrow," he said, looking at it from different angles. "Well, I'd better practice what I'm going to say: Good day, Your Majesty. Good *day*, Your *Majesty*!" Seeker straightened his shoulders and took a deep breath. "OK, here I go!"

He was just about to start up the path when suddenly he heard the voices of his friends, HopeSo, KnowSo, and Yes; Giggles, Gladness, and Glee; Dawdle and Slow; and Doodle and Do. As usual, Seeker's friends were with some of the CARNALville clowns. They all came running toward him, happily singing their song...

CARNALville! CARNALville! We love to go
To the CARNALville all day long!

Up and down, round and round,
Merrily go around,
We love the CARNALville so!

As long as he could remember, Seeker and the other children had sung that song. It was a happy, catchy little tune. It seemed so much fun to have all the candy and fun they wanted; but if any child had ever paused to look, or if they had stopped to really think about how selfish they were acting, they would have seen beyond the cheerful clown masks. They would have seen right through the disguise to some very wicked dragons hiding underneath the innocent-looking clown costumes. And they would have realized that the CARNALville clowns sang another song when the children weren't listening. It was a nasty little song:

This is the CARNALville of Selfishness
And we've got a hold of the Kingdom's Kids.
Aha, ha ha ha; Aha ha aha ha ha ha.
Aha ha aha ha ha ha.

Today the clowns whispered among themselves and picked their noses nervously as they watched the village children run toward Seeker.

Giggles called out happily, "Hi, Seeker. C'mon! We're going to the CARNALville!"

"A-a-are you c-c-coming, S-S-Seeker?" Dawdle and Slow asked together.

"Well, I should hope so!" HopeSo exclaimed.

"I know so!" said KnowSo.

"Yes, yes, of course he is!" Yes nodded vigorously.

Seeker answered a bit timidly, "Well, no. Actually, I'm not! I'm *not* going to the CARNALville today."

"What!" his friends cried loudly.

"What!" the clowns cried even louder. They had been

listening quietly, but now sprang into action. They pulled out their CARNALville balloons and candy, made sure their masks were in place, and hurried closer to the children. "Here is some yummy, yummy candy for you, kids," they smiled. "And remember, there's more and more and more candy waiting for you at the CARNALville today!"

The children grabbed handfuls of candy and stuffed their mouths full. But Seeker shook his head and pushed the clowns away. "I don't want any of your candy!" he said firmly. The clowns and the children were absolutely shocked. "No candy?"

"Wh-wh-what's wrong, S-S-Seeker?" Dawdle and Slow stuttered. "Are you s-s-sick or s-s-something?"

"Yes!" Seeker felt courage fill his heart. "I'm sick of that CARNALville! Sometimes those rides make my head hurt! And sometimes my stomach feels sick!"

The children responded, "But the candy tastes dandy. We don't think there can be anything better than it!"

Seeker squared his shoulders and responded, "Well, I think there could be! And I want to find out! I'm going to see the King...all by myself!"

"You're *what?*" the children cried, bewildered.

"You're *what?*" the clowns echoed. At the very mention of the King, their bodies began to tremble and they started to nervously pick their noses (which was quite difficult to do while wearing a mask).

Dawdle and Slow spoke up again, "C-c-c'mon, S-S-Seeker! We j-j-just had to go to that b-b-boring C-c-celebration yesterday!"

"Yeah!" HopeSo agreed. "C'mon, Seeker! What's wrong with you?"

"Nothing's wrong with *me!*" Seeker tried to explain. "I'm just starting to realize that the Kingdom is better than the CARNALville—and I'm going to see the King!" Seeker turned away from his friends, away from the CARNALville clowns, and started toward the castle once again.

But then, from beside the path, one of the clowns stuck his foot in the way and tripped Seeker, making him fall down! The clown pretended to be surprised, "Oh, you poor thing! What a nasty fall! Why don't you just sit down over here and have a bit of candy to help you feel better." The clown motioned to another clown who quickly offered Seeker some especially tasty candy.

"I don't want your candy!" he cried, pushing the candy away. As Seeker pushed, the clown was caught off balance and fell backward onto the ground; and as he fell, the clown mask shifted over to one side. Seeker saw the dark and slimy ugliness underneath the mask before the clown quickly set it back onto his face.

"Dragon!" Seeker shouted. "You aren't a clown at all. You're a dragon!" Seeker turned toward the other clown. "You!" Seeker cried. "You are another dragon!"

The children had huddled together, surprised by Seeker's burst of anger. Giggles was the first to speak. "Seeker," she giggled nervously, "you must have hit your head really hard when you fell! Are you all right?"

Glee laughed, "Seeker, come on. There aren't any dragons this close to the Kingdom! These are just clowns. That's all, just clowns."

The clowns waved and spoke in candy-coated voices. "That's right, boys and girls, we're just sweet little clowns!"

Seeker shook his head. "Dragons," he repeated. "They are dragons, and all you kids better get away from them!"

Gladness took one of the clowns by the hand and laughed. "Look at me, everybody! I'm holding on to a really bad dragon! I'm sure *glad* it doesn't bite!" The clown licked a lollipop innocently and the other children laughed.

"L-L-Let's get g-g-going to the CARNALville," Dawdle and Slow said together.

"Yes!" agreed Yes with a flip of her curls. "Let's leave Seeker alone. He needs to get busy. Maybe there are more dragons hiding around here for him to find!" Yes pretended to pick her nose and search for dragons. The other children laughed and began to pick their noses also, while making fun of Seeker.

"It's not funny," he whispered, biting back the tears that threatened to spill out. "The clowns are dragons! You need to be careful!" The children just laughed harder. The clowns made fun of Seeker, and some of the children, even his very best friends, called him names. It hurt Seeker inside, but he turned back toward the Straight and Narrow Path all by himself. "I don't care what you call me!" Seeker said, wiping away the tears that escaped from his eyes. "I'm going to see the King!" And with that, he began to run up the path toward the castle.

From the bottom of the hill, the clowns and children tried again to stop him. "The King is boring, Seeker!" they called. "Come with us to the CARNALville!" "We have candy for you, Seeker," called the clowns. "Lots and lots of candy!" As Seeker ran, the clowns and children continued to call out to him. He shut out their voices and focused on what he planned to say to the King, "Good day, Your Majesty! Good *day*, Your *Majesty!*" Finally, the clowns and children gave up and went on their way to the CARNALville of Selfishness.

Chapter Five

When Seeker reached the castle, he saw the Royal Doorkeeper standing in front of the door. It was a huge white door with beautiful gold trim. Above it, written in golden letters, were the words, "Whosoever will, may freely come." But Seeker wasn't looking at the words. His eyes were fixed on the Royal Doorkeeper, who seemed especially firm and official that day. "Who are you?" the Doorkeeper asked. "And what do you want?"

"My name is Seeker, and I want to see the King," Seeker answered, trying to sound confident.

The Doorkeeper leaned toward him, squinted his eyes in concentration, and spoke with a firm voice, "Do you *really* want to see the King?"

Seeker started to feel less confident. "Uh-huh," he responded hesitantly.

The Doorkeeper shook his head and folded his arms firmly. "No. You must *really* want to! Do you *really* want to?"

Seeker didn't answer right away. He was thinking. He was thinking about how the King had looked at him and how the King had winked at him. Seeker began to feel confident again. He squared his shoulders, took a deep breath, and answered the Royal Doorkeeper, "Yes sir, I *really* want to see the King!"

The Doorkeeper smiled and opened the castle door. "Great! Whosoever will—whoever *really* wants to—may freely come!" The Doorkeeper led Seeker into the castle.

Seeker's knees were trembling, and he could feel his heart pounding in his chest as he walked down the long shining hallway with the Doorkeeper. No thoughts of sliding came today as Seeker walked on that floor. All he could think of was seeing the King. "Good day, your Majesty. Good *day,* Your *Majesty!*" he practiced quietly.

When they reached the entrance to the Grand Throne Room, the Doorkeeper slowly opened the huge double doors. He bowed to the King and then stretched out his hand toward Seeker, motioning for the boy to enter the Throne Room. The Doorkeeper then stepped back, and Seeker went, all by himself, into the presence of the King.

Seeker stared at the floor as he slowly walked toward the throne. He had never been in that room before except for the weekly Celebration. Today, there was no laughter and music of the villagers, no happy clanging of dishes of food being passed around. The only sound in the Grand Throne Room was Seeker's beating heart, his footsteps approaching the throne, and the bubbling of water in the fountain. Finally, he stood before the King, holding his hands together anxiously. A long moment passed. When Seeker finally felt enough courage to look up, he was surprised and relieved to see the King smiling at him. It was a very gentle, happy smile. Seeker smiled back, and then remembered his manners. He knelt down, cleared his throat, took a deep breath, and started to recite his practiced greeting.

"Good d—" Something about the way the King was smiling at him made Seeker stop. He waited just a moment and then, before he had time to think about it, he said, "Hi." The word just came out of Seeker's mouth. He felt embarrassed. Why did he do that? You don't just say, "Hi" to a king! But the King smiled an even bigger smile and said, *"Hi."*

There was a brief silence, then Seeker looked up again. "My name is Seeker," he said softly.

The King bent closer, looked right into Seeker's eyes, and said just as softly, "I *know.*"

Seeker looked deep into the King's kind eyes and spoke with all his heart, "I *really* want to get to know you."

The King bent closer yet and said with all *his* heart, "I *know.* Come on, Seeker, I will show you my castle!"

"Show me your castle?" Seeker echoed, his eyes getting large and excited. "You mean you will really show me your castle?"

The King laughed. "Yes! And the first place we will go is right down the shining hallway!" They walked across the Grand Throne Room and stood together at the end of the shining hallway. The King leaned over and spoke very seriously, "Take off your shoes, Seeker."

Seeker wondered if the King was worried about him scratching the floor or something. Without questioning, he took off his shoes.

To Seeker's utter amazement, the King took off his shoes, too! Then, very seriously, but with laughter twinkling from his eyes, the King reached out and took hold of Seeker's hand.

"Shall we?" said the King, and off they went—sliding down the shining hallway!

This was far better than any dream Seeker had ever dreamed; he had never imagined himself sliding on the shining hallway with the King! Up and down and back and forth they slid. The castle servants came and watched the King and Seeker and shook their heads in amazement, "We've never seen him act like this before!" they said to each other. The King looked at their expressions and laughed. He laughed and laughed and laughed. The sound of his laughter echoed past the castle halls, down the hill, and through the streets of Peace and Harmony. Villagers looked up from their work as a delighted shiver briefly overtook them. The King's laughter continued to echo until it reached the CARNALville of Selfishness. Suddenly, the candy the children were eating didn't taste as good as it used to taste, and the rides didn't seem as exciting. The children held their stomachs, looked around, and realized that they felt very, very empty inside.

Meanwhile, back at the castle, the King stretched out his hand to Seeker again. "That was fun!" he said. "Let's slide some more!" After awhile the King took Seeker on a tour of the Castle. They slid down other shining hallways, climbed up into secret towers, and ran down winding staircases. They explored some of the deep, mysterious parts of the castle. Seeker's favorite discovery was an underground waterfall. The spray of water on his face felt delicious and alive.

Then the King ordered a royal picnic lunch to be prepared. He and Seeker ate together beside the stream at the base of the Straight and Narrow Path. They spent the afternoon there, skipping rocks across the water and fishing. The King explained how water from the Grand Throne Room fountain tumbled down the underground waterfall and flowed out into the stream, where everyone in the Kingdom could enjoy the clear fresh water. Seeker had a big drink of the sparkling water and listened intently all afternoon as the King told him wonderful stories about his Kingdom.

Chapter Six

When Seeker left the King's Castle that night, he was so tired that he immediately fell asleep. The rooster had to crow *really* loudly the next morning to wake him up. Seeker jumped out of bed, got dressed, ran downstairs, ate his breakfast, and headed for the door. His mother was standing there like she had the previous morning, smiling and holding his toothbrush. "Oops! Forgot about my teeth again!" Seeker quickly brushed his teeth and then hugged his mother. But today, it wasn't the usual little hug. Today, Seeker hugged her so hard that she gasped in surprise. "Bye, Mom!" he said, excitement shining from his eyes. "I'm going to see the King!"

"All by yourself," Contentment said with a smile. She waved goodbye and then stood leaning in the doorway, watching Seeker race toward the Straight and Narrow Path. A deep happiness washed through Contentment's heart as she thought about her son *really* getting to know the King. "I never realized what *true* contentment was," she whispered to herself, "until now."

Seeker reached the path and came to a screeching halt. To his surprise, all his friends were there. HopeSo, KnowSo, and Yes; Giggles, Gladness, and Glee; Dawdle and Slow; and Doodle and Do stood waiting for him at the Big Rock. The CARNALville clowns were busily trying to hand out candy and balloons, but the children kept pushing them away. Seeker's friends were acting very strangely, and much to the clowns' dismay, they were acting completely and utterly bored.

CARNALville, CARNALville, we love to go
To the CARNALville all day long

Up and down, round and round,
merrily go around
We love the CARNALville so
But sometimes those rides make my head hurt
And sometimes my stomach feels sick;
But the candy tastes dandy—
I don't think there can be anything better than it....

Seeker hurried to his friends and said, "Oh, yes there is! There is some*one* better! The King! He is *much* better! He's wonderful!"

"He is?" the children asked together.

The clowns frantically offered candy and balloons, desperately trying to distract the children and cover their ears so they wouldn't hear what Seeker was saying. (This was all quite difficult for the clowns to do because they were trembling with fear at the very mention of the King. In fact, they were shaking so badly they could hardly pick their noses!)

"Yes, the King is wonderful!" Seeker responded with excitement. "I had the best day of my whole life yesterday, and I'm going again today!" Seeker stepped onto the Straight and Narrow Path, then turned back to the other children. "Hey, I just got an idea! Why don't you all come with me to see the King!"

Quickly, the clowns pushed their way between Seeker and his friends. They offered more candy and balloons. They held out free tickets to the CARNALville rides, but the children ignored them. "To see the King! You mean we could?"

"Sure!" Seeker answered. He pushed the clowns back with a strength that surprised everyone, especially himself. The clowns whined and whimpered in pain. Seeker stepped closer to his friends, and then continued soberly, "If you *really* want to! Do you *really* want to?"

The children nodded. "Uh-huh."

Seeker shook his head and folded his arms firmly. "Uh-uh! You must really want to! Do you really want to? Get that straight because they ask it all the time!"

"Yes!" the children cried.

"The CARNALville just doesn't make me giggle anymore, and Seeker, you look so happy!" Giggles said.

The others agreed. "Yes! We really want to get to know the King!"

The clowns had recovered from Seeker's push, and now they moved close again. They began to speak in their most candy-coated voices, "Boys and girls, of course you don't really want to get to know the King! The King is boring, remember? Come with us. We have more of our very own special secret recipe candy for you!"

"No!" the children cried together. "We don't want any of your candy!"

The clowns pretended to have hurt feelings. "No candy?" they whined. "But it's so good for you! Here, try this piece. It's from our brand-new especially most secret recipe." The clowns held out brightly-colored, swirled candy sticks.

Doodle and Do looked at each other. "Do you think we should try one little piece?"

Dawdle and Slow protectively stepped in front of Doodle and Do and spoke forcefully at the clowns, "D-D-Didn't you hear us or s-s-something? We don't want your candy!"

"But it's very good candy," one clown said sweetly. "Try it." The clown reached out with a stick of candy. Dawdle brushed it aside, and as he did, the edge of the stick caught on the clown's mask and pulled it off.

The children stared in horror at the ugly, slimy, dark face. "Dragon!"

"Seeker was right!" KnowSo cried. "Let's get out of here!"

The dragon-clowns stepped forward again with their candy and balloons. "Wait! OK, OK, so you found us out. Listen, kids, sure we're dragons, but we're really nice dragons! We won't hurt you! Now c'mon and have some candy."

Seeker again pushed the dragon-clowns. This time he pushed so hard that they fell down on the ground, whimpering loudly. All the children looked at Seeker with great respect and admiration. "How did you do that?" Doodle asked, as they all walked toward the path.

"I'm not sure," Seeker answered. "But I think it's because I was with the King all day yesterday! And my mom told me about a weapon that..."

"L-L-Look out, Seeker!" Slow cried and pointed behind him. "D-D-Dragons!"

Seeker turned to face the dragons. They had gotten up from the ground, thrown off their clown disguises, and were now rushing toward Seeker in full-force dragon rage. But Seeker wasn't afraid. He remembered the words from the song; he remembered the powerful weapon. He stood very tall and yelled, "In the King's name, you get out of here!"

The effect was amazing. It was like an invisible lightning bolt hit the dragons. They flew backward through the air and landed with a loud thump. They held their bodies and rolled on the ground, screaming with pain.

Seeker grabbed his friends by the hand and whirled back toward the Straight and Narrow Path. "Come on everybody! Let's go!"

"No! No!" the dragons shouted as they tried to get up. "Listen, kids, you can have free lifetime passes to every ride! We'll even give you the recipe for the candy! Come back! Come back!" But none of the children listened; instead, they all ran toward the castle with Seeker.

The clowns angrily stomped on their balloons, shoved the candy back into their pockets, and picked their noses all the way back to the CARNALville; all the way back to their master in the deep, dark place beneath the trap door of Selfishness.

Chapter Seven

The Royal Doorkeeper was very surprised to see all the children standing before him at the entrance to the castle. "Who are you?" he asked firmly. "And what do you want?"

"We're the kids!" came the energetic reply. "And we want to see the King!" The children leaned toward the Doorkeeper convincingly. "We *really* want to see the King!"

The Doorkeeper smiled and opened the castle door. "Great! Then come with me!" The Doorkeeper led the children into the castle and down the shining hallway. When Seeker told his friends how he and the King had gone sliding down the hallway, their eyes grew huge in wonder.

When they reached the entrance to the Grand Throne Room, the Doorkeeper slowly opened the huge double doors. He bowed to the King and then stretched out his hand toward the children, motioning for them to enter the Grand Throne Room. The Doorkeeper then stepped back, and the children of the Kingdom went into the presence of the King.

Seeker half-ran and half-slid across the Grand Throne Room floor into the King's great arms. The King lifted Seeker high into the air and twirled him around in circles, laughing. HopeSo, KnowSo, and Yes; Giggles, Gladness, and Glee; Dawdle and Slow; and Doodle and Do watched with open mouths and wonder in their eyes. This was a side of the King they never knew existed.

They watched as the King finally put Seeker back down on the floor and turned his attention toward them. The King smiled at them. It was a very gentle, happy smile. The children smiled back and then remembered their manners. They knelt down and looked up into the King's eyes. A few moments passed.

"Just say, 'Hi,'" Seeker encouraged his friends.

The children smiled shyly at the King. "Hi," they said.

The King smiled, and responded with a warm, *"Hi."*

"We're the kids," they said softly.

The King bent closer, looked into their eyes, and said just as softly, "I *know.*"

The children looked deep into the King's kind eyes and spoke with all their hearts, "We really want to get to know you."

The King bent closer yet and said with all his heart, "I *know.*"

Then the King laughed a great laugh. The sound of his laughter echoed past the castle halls, down the hill, and through the streets of Peace and Harmony. Villagers looked up from their work as a delighted shiver briefly overtook them. The King's laughter continued to echo until it reached the CARNALville of Selfishness, where the dragon-clowns shook in violent fear at the sound and once again felt pain from where the child, Seeker, had pushed them back with the King's name.

"Come," the King said to the children, "I will show you my castle!"

And that was the beginning...of adventures in the Kingdom.

Think About the Story

The best part about this story is that it is true! There truly is a Kingdom of Joy and Peace, and there truly is a King. His name is Jesus. You can get to know Him—if you really want to. You can spend time with King Jesus every day. Just say His name and He will hear you.

Talk to the King

"King Jesus, I don't want to live my life at the CARNALville of Selfishness, trying to always please myself. I want to be like Seeker and really get to know You. Today I ask You to be the King and Ruler of my life!"

Read from the King's Great Book—Daniel 11:32B

*The people who **know** their King will be strong on the inside and go adventuring!* (Daniel 11:32b, Great Book Paraphrase)

Part Two

Rescued from the Dragon

Chapter One

The laughter of children poured out from the castle walls and echoed throughout the Village of Peace and Harmony. Villagers looked up from their work and smiled. Their children loved spending time with the King. It used to be that those same children needed to be coaxed to go to the King's Celebration once a week, but now they ran up the Straight and Narrow Path to the castle every morning. Seeker and his friends were now seeking to know more about the King.

And today there was another kind of seeking going on. The children had spent several hours sliding down the shining castle hallways and playing in the underground waterfall, but now they were in the castle's Royal Courtyard playing a game of hide and seek, and the King was "it."

The King had been playing the game with a lot of energy, when he suddenly looked very, very sad. He went and sat down on a bench, and the children gathered around him. The expression on his face made the children feel worried.

"Are you all right, King?" Seeker asked. "What's the matter?"

The King smiled a sad smile and answered, "Thank you for your concern...but I'm fine..."

"D-d-don't you l-l-like playing hide and seek, King?" Dawdle asked.

"A-a-aren't you having fun, King?" Slow asked, patting the King's shoulder.

An even greater sadness filled the King's expression. "Sometimes," he said quietly, "seeking for people who are hiding is not very much fun."

The children were puzzled. "What *do* you mean?" asked Doodle. "You can always find us, King! You just pretend not to know where we are!"

The King smiled. "I can find you because you want me to. But...there are some people who don't want me to find them." When he said that the King leaned back in the bench and his sadness was so great that the children felt like crying.

Seeker watched the King, wondering. There was something familiar about the King's sadness...something very familiar.... The other children were startled when suddenly Seeker cried out, "Now I remember! Hey, King! You looked sad that other day, too!"

The King appeared puzzled. "What other day, Seeker?"

"You know—that other day!" said Seeker, "That day at the Celebration! The day you winked at me during the banquet!"

"Oh..." replied the King, "You mean like this?" He leaned forward and winked. Seeker and the other children laughed.

"Uh-huh!" answered Seeker. "Well, that day you were looking at the third banquet table—you know, the empty one, and you were looking so sad. Why were you sad that day, King?"

"And why *do* you look so sad today, King?" Do asked sincerely.

The King looked at the eager young faces around him and said, "Do you *really* want to know? The reason I am sad means very much to me...and I can't tell you about it unless you *really* want to know."

"We want to know, King!" the children said with all their hearts. "We *really* want to know!"

"All right, then; I'll show you!" The King stood to his feet and pointed at one of the castle towers. "Come—we have to climb the Lookout Tower."

Chapter Two

Seeker and his friends followed the King through the wooden door of Lookout Tower and down a wide hallway where the royal building supplies were kept. Giggles, Gladness, and Glee playfully danced with the paint cans and mops and hoes before climbing up the tower's winding stone staircase.

Lookout Tower takes some people quite a long time to climb, but the Kingdom children quickly reached the top. "Wow!" exclaimed Giggles. "You can see for miles up here!"

Gladness pointed, "There's Peace and Harmony!"

"Look!" shouted Glee, "There's our house!"

"And look over there!" Seeker said. "There's that old selfish CARNALville. It sure looks small from up here!"

Everyone agreed. After a few moments, while the other children kept talking and pointing excitedly, Dawdle and Slow remembered why they had climbed the tower. They turned to the King, "D-d-does this t-t-tower make you s-s-sad, King?"

"No," the King answered, "the tower doesn't make me sad— it's what you can see from the tower. Look—way over there! Tell me what you see."

The children looked off into the distance, and they saw a dark, gloomy village. And as they looked harder, they could see it more and more clearly. (Seeing more clearly is what happens when the King shows you something from Lookout Tower.) The village had walls around it, but the walls were broken down. There was garbage everywhere and junk was piled up almost as high as the roofs of the buildings. The houses looked as though they hadn't been cleaned or painted for a very long time. Weeds were growing instead of flowers, the trees had bare branches without leaves, and the lawns looked like they had never seen a lawnmower.

The children looked even more closely...trying to see if anyone actually lived in the village. Then Seeker pointed and yelled, "Look! There at the gate—a dragon! A great big dragon!"

"Oh, yuck!" cried Giggles. "It's picking its nose!"

"That is so disgusting!" Yes said, standing closer to the King.

"That is so gross!" Glee said.

"That is so nauseating," KnowSo stated, holding his stomach.

"That," the King said sadly, "is...the dragon Greed."

The tone of his voice made the children turn to him soberly. "The dragon...Greed. Is that what's been making you feel sad, King?"

The King nodded. "Very, very sad. The dragon Greed is the ruler of the Village Greed. He breathes thoughts into the people's minds continually—thoughts of getting and having and never sharing. I love those people so much! I want them to come to the Celebration and eat at my banquet! I want to bring them out of Greed and into my Kingdom!"

Seeker nodded, understanding now. "Hide and seek...you want to *find* those people."

Do moved closer to the King and asked earnestly, "Then, why don't you *do* it, King?"

"Yeah, King, rescue them just like you rescued our families from the Dragon Fear!" Seeker turned to explain to his friends. "It happened a long time ago. My mom told me all about it."

"Rescue them from Greed just like how you rescued us from the CARNALville!" HopeSo said, and the other children nodded, remembering.

Just then the King quickly reached forward and pulled Yes

away from the edge of the Tower. She had been leaning too far forward and was about to lose her balance. "Yes!" she cried in relief. "Those people need to be rescued! Whew!"

The King nodded. "I want to rescue them. I want to set them free from the dragon's power; I want to *find* them...but they don't *really* want me to! They like being greedy..."

"They like it?" echoed the children in surprise.

"That's awful!" exclaimed HopeSo.

"That's terrible!" agreed KnowSo.

"Th-th-that's sad," Dawdle and Slow said together.

The King nodded, "Yes, it is sad. The people like being greedy; and they have heard that if they come into my Kingdom, I would take everything away from them, and I wouldn't give them anything."

The children were shocked. "You wouldn't do that, King!" said Seeker. "You don't love to get—you love to give!"

"You know that, Seeker, and I know that..."

"But they don't know that!" the children shook their heads together.

"What I need," the King continued, "is someone to go and tell them the truth about me!"

The children leaned thoughtfully along the tower ledge. "I wonder who could go tell them about the King?"

"Hmm..." said the King, looking at all of the children, "I wonder?"

Suddenly, Giggles said, "I have an idea, King! Send a messenger!"

The King shook his head. "I've tried that."

The children looked at each other, shrugged their shoulders, and then leaned thoughtfully along the tower ledge again. "He's tried that."

"Hey!" Gladness said eagerly, "How about having a big party and inviting them to come!"

The King shook his head again, "They're not interested."

"They're not interested," the children echoed sadly, shrugged their shoulders, and again leaned thoughtfully on the tower ledge.

"There has to be something you could *do*, King!" Doodle said.

"I *know*, King!" KnowSo spoke up excitedly. "How about an army?"

"Yes! An army!" Yes cried.

All of the children began to imagine a great army of fine Kingdom soldiers marching toward Greed and conquering the fierce dragon.

Do slipped his hand into the King's and asked hopefully, "*Do* you *have* an army, King?"

The King smiled a mysterious smile, "Yes...a little one."

Doodle felt discouraged, "It's not very big, eh?"

"Hmm..." the King continued to smile mysteriously, "I think it's big enough."

"W-w-where is your army, K-K-King?" Dawdle and Slow asked, "C-c-can we see it?"

"It's not far away! In fact, it is very, very close," said the King. "Close your eyes real tight...and I'll show it to you!"

The King gently took hold of each child by the shoulders and turned them slowly. "OK, you stand here. And I'll put you right there. Keep your eyes shut, now! OK, and you over here." The King lined the children up in a circle so they were facing each other. "There! Now open your eyes and see my army!"

"What!" The children were absolutely shocked. They pointed and cried, "Him? Her! Us! We are your army, King? Really!?"

Seeker and his friends were very quiet for a moment; then they all said together at exactly the same time, "Uh-oh."

The King laughed a deep, happy laugh. "Why are you so surprised? I have chosen you, and you are my army. You will go to the Village Greed and tell the people there the truth about me! You will be my powerful Kingdom soldiers!"

The children were very quiet for another moment; then again they all said together at exactly the same time, "Uh-oh."

"Come on," said the King. "Let's go back down to the courtyard."

The children quietly followed the King back down the winding stone steps of the Lookout Tower. No one spoke because each child was thinking about what the King had showed them.

Chapter Three

When they reached the castle courtyard, the children sat down. Finally, after several moments, Seeker broke the silence and said what all of the children had been thinking, "You know, King, I don't think we can do this. We're just kids!"

"We want to tell those people who live in Greed the truth about you, King," Doodle said. "We *really do*; but they wouldn't listen to us. We're just kids!"

"Just kids?" the King repeated. "In my army, age has nothing to do with whether or not a person is a good soldier." The children looked at him doubtfully, and the King continued, "In fact, here in my Kingdom, someone who appears to be young and small can actually become the most powerful!"

The children looked at the King, trying to believe him. Then Do sadly shook his head, "Sorry, King. We just can't *do* it!"

"I just *know* they wouldn't listen to us, King!" KnowSo said.

The King laughed again. "It will take some time, and it will take some work...but you *can* do it! They will listen to you!"

"B-b-but...wh-wh-what about the d-d-dragon?" cried Dawdle and Slow.

"Yeah!" agreed the children. "What about the dragon?"

Yes moved closer to the King. "Yes," she said, "What about the dragon? It's a very big dragon, King."

"The dragon appears to be big," nodded the King, motioning for the children to come closer, "but he can only be as big as you let him be. I will teach you a song to sing to the dragon Greed, and the song will make him lose his strength! Listen carefully now, this is the song:

> *We don't love to get, we love to give!*
> *We don't love to get, we love to give!*
> *Serving the King has made us sing,*
> *And loving the King means everything!*
> *We don't love to get, we love to give!*

The King repeated the song several times and the children learned it quickly. As they sang along, courage filled their hearts, and no dragon seemed big enough to ever be able to stop them. When the children finished singing, they bowed and curtsied, and the King applauded. "You must go to the Village Greed in a spirit of generosity!" he said.

The children looked at the King, puzzled. "Wh-wh-what's g-g-generosity mean?" asked Dawdle and Slow.

"It means *loving* to give!" the King answered. "Give your time, give your service, give, give, *give!*"

The children were puzzled. "But King, what can we give? We're just kids!"

The King acted surprised. "Just kids?" The children smiled, embarrassed that they had so quickly forgotten that age didn't matter in the King's army. The King picked up a rake that was leaning against one of the courtyard walls. "Alright, soldiers, here are the kinds of tools you need to defeat the dragon Greed! You will overcome greed with—giving!"

Giggles, Gladness, and Glee caught on right away. They ran through the door of Lookout Tower and came back with hoes and brooms, buckets, and cans of paint.

"We can take hoes to hoe their gardens; brooms to sweep their floors!" Glee announced brightly.

"Soap to wash their windows, and paint to paint their doors!" Giggles laughed at the rhyme.

"I will mop the floors until they shine like new!" said Gladness, laughing.

"Mowing lawns is something that I like to *do*!" said Doodle.

"I *hope* I can take Mom's homemade bread!"

"Uh, uh..." KnowSo scrambled to find a rhyme, then smiled. "I *know* she wants the people *fed!*"

The other children laughed and slapped KnowSo on the back. Then they stopped laughing when they realized the King was watching them with one of his mysterious smiles.

"Good," nodded the King, "Very good. You shall overcome greed with giving! And every kind thing that you do, no matter how small it might seem, will be powerful against the dragon." The King motioned to the children to come close to him.

"When you go to the Village Greed, I want you to tell them the truth about me. I want you to take an important message to them...a most important message." As he said those words, the King became sad again. It was like a great weight settled upon his heart. The children gathered around him quietly, and the King spoke to them with such sadness that again they felt as though they would cry with him.

"What is your message, King? What do you want us to tell them?"

The King looked around at the children's faces and whispered, "Tell them...that I love them."

> *Tell them there's a King who loves them.*
> *Tell them there's a King who cares!*
> *Tell them there's a King...Who loves them—*
> *A King who gives and shares!*
> *I want to give to them new life in my Kingdom;*
> *I want to give them my joy and my peace.*
> *I will fill their hearts with happiness and laughter*
> *As they really get to know me.*

"We'll tell them, King," the children said sincerely. "We'll tell them."

Then the King stood up and spoke in his most kingly voice, "Alright then, you are my army! Giggles, Gladness, and Glee," the three children turned quickly when the King called their names, "I want you especially to remember the song about giving. Be ready to cheer on the troops!"

Giggles, Gladness, and Glee stood like soldiers and saluted as they sang, "We don't love to get, we love to give, sir!"

"Dawdle and Slow, Doodle and Do!" When the King called their names, the children stood at attention. "*Do* your best!"

"Yes sir! We'll *do* it, sir!"

"HopeSo, KnowSo, and Yes—do not be afraid; you will be fine soldiers!"

"I *hope* so, sir!"

"I *know* so, sir!"

"Yes, yes of course we will, sir!"

"Seeker!" Seeker saluted and stood ready to hear the King's words. "You shall lead the troops!"

"Yes, sir!"

"It's going to take work, and it's going to take discipline!" the King said as he walked up and down the line of soldiers. "Now, go home, get a good night's sleep, and report for duty at sunrise!"

"Yes, sir!"

Then the King saluted with a wink, and went into the castle.

The children continued to stand at attention. Do asked the question they were all wondering. "*Do* you think we're really the King's army?"

"I *hope* so!"

"I *know* so!"

"Yes, yes of course we are!"

Seeker took a step forward in front of the line and shouted,

"Report for duty at sunrise! On with the adventure!" And the children of the Kingdom marched out from the castle court-yard, down the Straight and Narrow Path, and back to their homes in Peace and Harmony. They had a lot of work to do before the next morning.

Chapter Four

Early the next morning, near the forests of Laws Forgotten, the crow of a grouchy rooster filled the air. The dragon Greed stretched and groaned and stood to his feet in front of his village gate. With a loud belch of breath that smelled like rotten eggs, the dragon began to sing, as he did every morning, to an imaginary audience:

> *I am the dragon, the dragon Greed!*
> *I rule this town—it is named after ME!*
> *I breathe lovely thoughts to my people —*
> *Dreams and dark ambitions;*
> *I fill their heads with greediness,*
> *And lots of selfish wishes.*
> *They are under my control—*
> *I'm the one who feeds them!*
> *Yet, the yearning in their souls*
> *never, never leaves them!*

Just then, the people of Greed came through the gate to report to the dragon. He laughed a very wicked laugh and picked his nose rudely while going over the list of Greed citizens in an off-key, sing-song voice. "First, there's the mayor, Mayor Miser the Mad. His wife is ungrateful; she's snobbish and Mad."

"I'm Just Mad!" the mayor's wife screeched so loudly that everyone around her cowered in alarm.

Delighted, the dragon rubbed his claws together and continued, "Their offspring make my greedy heart glad; their names are Stingy, Persnickety, and Just Bad!"

Just Bad stepped forward and stuck his tongue out at the dragon, "I'm Just Bad!" he declared.

The dragon chuckled and patted the boy's head. Then went on in his list of citizens: "Baker Moocha More-eh, his wife Mucha More-eh, and their uh....*charming* young daughter, Megga More-eh."

Mucha More-eh stuffed her mouth so full of doughnuts that she choked. Just Bad pointed and cried, "Ugh! She is disgusting!" At this remark, Mucha threw doughnut crumbs in Just Mad's face and the daily fighting began.

The dragon crooned happily and went over to two women dressed in fine clothing. They were whispering gossip about the other Greed citizens, and fanning themselves proudly. "Ahhh," said the dragon in his sing-song voice, "Auntie Ambition and Fanciful, two favorites of mine—dreaming and scheming and wasting their time! They love to tell stories and their stories are *all*...lies!"

The people of Greed were all very greedy, but in a variety of ways. Mayor Miser the Mad and his wife, Just Mad, were greedy for fame and power. They loved being the most important people in the village, and they felt as though everyone else should serve them. Their children, Stingy, Persnickety, and Just Bad greedily asked for games and toys and new clothes all the time, but when they got those things, they were only happy for a few minutes. Then they wanted something else.

Baker Moocha More-eh, and his wife, Mucha More-eh, and their daughter, Megga More-eh, were greedy for food. But no matter how much they ate, they never felt full inside. Auntie Ambition and Fanciful were greedy for attention and liked to wear clothing and makeup that made people look at them. They spent hours dreaming and scheming and wasting their time, making up stories about their fellow citizens as well as endless stories of their own travels and achievements, but none of their stories were true.

The dragon sauntered over to a ragged-looking family. This family was very greedy about having things that weren't theirs to have. They were dressed in filthy, torn clothes, and they smelled so badly that even the dragon plugged his nose to cover the stench as he spoke their names. "Mr. and Mrs. Smudge Yukerty, the town cleaning crew, they keep the village looking like...new!"

Smudge stepped forward and boasted about his three little sons, "Dark, Dingy, and Dirty take after me! They help earn extra money...by stealing things!" Smudge proudly held up a gold pocket watch and fine string of pearls for all to see.

Mayor Miser the Mad and his wife, Just Mad, gasped and screamed, "My gold watch!" "My pearls!"

The dragon Greed stepped between the two families, shielding the three little boys protectively. "Now, now, now," he spoke soothingly, "Let's just sing the Old Town Song, shall we?" The villagers immediately forgot their disagreements. They were proud of the song and sang it together with great enthusiasm.

> *We've—gathered up riches and wealth*
> *and things we're not about to part with!*
> *Greedily gathered and grabbed at things;*
> *We've been so wonderfully selfish!*
> *Our village has a name to uphold;*
> *A reputation have we;*
> *For miles around our fame is renowned;*
> *We're known as the people Greed*
> *(Hee-hee-hee-hee-hee!)*

The people of the Village Greed lived a terrible life of arguing, fighting, stealing, and always wanting more. And no one, especially the dragon, was expecting anything to ever change. And no one, especially the dragon, knew that at that very moment, an army was approaching the village.

Chapter Five

Yes, an army was approaching the village, an army of children. They were carrying hoes, rakes, brooms, mops, cans of paint, and boxes filled with good things to give and share; and they were marching on a path the King had made through the forests north of the World Beyond the Kingdom.

"Look—there's the CARNALville!" pointed Gladness. "I'm sure *glad* we don't go there anymore!"

"Just keep marching," Seeker warned. "Don't stop and don't even look at the CARNALville. We don't want to meet up with any dragon-clowns today!"

The others agreed and kept marching steadily toward Greed. It was mid-morning when they arrived at the outskirts of the village. Swarms of flies buzzed around the village walls. Odd looking trees without leaves were trying to grow along the path, together with weeds and tall brown grasses. The stench was incredible. The smell of rotten eggs swirled around the children. "Ugh!" Glee cried, holding her nose. "Where is that terrible smell coming from?"

"Next time, let's bring some air freshener!" Giggles said, coughing.

"And bug spray!" Glee said, trying to wave away some flies.

"Shhh!" Seeker pointed with an excited whisper. "Look! *That's* where the smell is coming from!"

"Dragon!" the children were horrified. "The dragon Greed."

"L-l-ooks even b-b-bigger close up...d-d-doesn't he?" stammered Dawdle and Slow.

Seeker put a warning finger to his lips, "Shh!"

Do peeked out from behind Seeker's back. "*Do* you think he's sleeping?"

"Well, there's only one way to find out!" whispered Doodle. "Go ahead, Do!"

"Me?" whispered Do loudly. "No way! You *do* it, Doodle!"

Doodle pushed his brother forward, "You can *do* it, Do!"

Do stepped back and pushed his brother forward, "C'mon, Doodle—*do* it!"

Seeker firmly stepped in front of them. "*I'll* do it! You all wait here! It looks like that gate is the only entrance to the village; I'll try to sneak around the dragon..."

The children called after him in anxious whispers, "Be careful, Seeker!"

Seeker moved bravely and carefully toward the dragon. Closer and closer, until he was almost close enough to touch the great beast. Seeker held his nose and tried to keep from getting sick. The dragon's breath was terrible, and he smelled as though he had never, ever brushed his teeth and never, ever taken a bath. Seeker pinched his nose tightly and began to step toward the entrance gate of the village. But suddenly...!

"ROAR!" The dragon stood up with a loud and vicious howl!

The dragon Greed towered over Seeker, whose legs were shaking violently. The dragon shouted, and his voice rumbled throughout the countryside. The rats and slimy crawling creatures scurried for cover. Even the flies buzzed away, fearfully trying to find a hiding place. "Who dares to approach Greed—unannounced! Uninvited!" the dragon shouted, his terrible breath rushing at Seeker and his mouth dripping with disgusting green slobber. "Speak up, you, or I'll turn you into a heap of smoldering ashes!"

Seeker wiped drips of disgusting slobber from his arm and frantically called to his friends, "Wh-what was the song? What was the song we're supposed to sing to the dragon!"

Giggles, Gladness, and Glee gulped. They remembered the song, but what good would it do against this terrible creature? Then the dragon reached an ugly clawed hand toward Seeker, and Seeker called out again, "Hurry! What was the song!"

Giggles, Gladness, and Glee tried to call, but they were so afraid that the song just came out of their lips like a little whisper, "We don't love to get...we love to give."

Instantly, the dragon winced in pain and turned his attention to Giggles, Gladness, and Glee. "I beg your pardon," he sneered, *"What* did you say?"

Giggles, Gladness, and Glee gulped in fear and whispered again, "We don't love to get...we love to give."

The dragon winced again and put his clawed hands over his ears. "Get away from here. Go away with your feeble little tune!"

Giggles, Gladness, and Glee repeated the words of the song, and the other children joined in, gradually singing louder and more confidently as they watched what the song did to the dragon. He was holding his ears and squirming in pain. "Go away, you bad and nasty children!" The dragon growled as he stood protectively in front of the village gate. "Go away! That is a terrible song! A terrible song!" But the children just sang more loudly:

> *"We don't love to get, we love to give!*
> *We don't love to get, we love to give!*
> *'Cause serving the King has made us sing!*
> *And loving the King means everything!*
> *We don't love to get, we love to give!"*

"Serving the King has made you sing?" The dragon Greed whined, cried, and then howled in a fit of rage. "Don't mention him around here! Bad and nasty King! Go away you bad and nasty children! Go away!"

"Sing again, louder this time," Seeker called.

The dragon roared in anger, held his ears, and shook his head back and forth in agony. He tried to shut out the song by grabbing a nearby trash can and pulling it over his head, but the children just sang louder and moved forward. The closer the children came, the more agony the dragon was in, and he seemed to get smaller. "Look!" cried Seeker. "He's shrinking! Sing louder, everyone! Sing louder!"

Sure enough, the dragon was shrinking, and the song had pushed him back so the entrance gate to Greed was no longer blocked. The children saw what was happening. "Hurry!" they cried. "Go through the gate!" Still singing with all their strength, the army of children ran past the miserable dragon and into the Village Greed.

Glee turned and pointed at the dragon as she ran through the gate, "We're not bad and nasty children! *You* are a very bad and very nasty dragon! And the people who live here are about to know the *truth* about the King!"

"No! No!" the dragon cried desperately. "You can't go in there! It's *my* village! They belong to me! Don't tell them about the King! No! No!" He fell in front of the gate sobbing loudly. "No! Don't tell them about the King!"

But much to the dragon's anger, the children from the Kingdom of Joy and Peace were already in the Village Greed. And they were already at work—singing, sharing, giving, and telling the people the truth about the King who loved them.

Chapter Six

S eeker and his friends kept visiting the Village Greed every day. The children began each morning by spending time with the King, and then off they marched, singing their songs. Gradually the dragon Greed had become weaker and weaker, until he could no longer guard the door; and when he saw the Kingdom children, all he could do was moan a pitiful moan.

The people of Greed were concerned, very concerned. One day all of the villagers were called to attend a Town Council Meeting—all of the people except the Greed children, that is; they weren't invited. (But if anyone had been watching closely, they might have noticed Dark, Dingy, and Dirty; Stingy, Persnickety, and Just Bad; and the baker's daughter, Megga, sneaking underneath the tablecloth, where no one could see them!)

Everyone chattered in concerned, anxious voices as they took their places at the Town Council table.

Mayor Miser the Mad pounded the table to get everyone's attention. He cleared his throat and spoke in his most dramatic voice, "This emergency meeting was called tonight to decide what we're going to do. These kids, they keep coming—they're giving and loving—we just don't know quite what they're up to!"

Just Mad stood to her feet. "I'm in a state of frustration, and I'm losing my patience!" she wailed. "And it's all because of these kids!"

(Beneath the table, the mayor's son, Just Bad, was in trouble. He was allergic to flour and he was hiding right beside

Baker Moocha More-eh. Each time the baker moved, clouds of flour settled under the table. Just Bad was struggling not to sneeze.)

Auntie Ambition stood to speak, fanning herself dramatically, "Their singing and bringing have set our heads spinning—we can't understand these kids!"

Smudge Yukerty spoke with deep concern, "The dragon's power is weakening—it always seems he's sleeping, and hardly guarding the door..."

"I've noticed he's not eating; that's sure not in keeping," said the baker slowly. "And I've hardly heard him roar!"

At that very moment a low and painful moan was heard. (Everyone thought it was the dragon, but it was actually Just Bad, still trying his best not to sneeze.)

"There, now, you heard that!" the baker said. "The dragon's sick, and that's a fact!"

Mrs. Yukerty stood to her feet, crying, "The streets have been clean-swept; the houses have been up-kept; even the doors have been painted! All my windows are shining, my floors aren't so grimy, and there aren't any weeds in my garden!" She sat back down, sobbing and wailing.

Smudge put his arm around his wife and then said, "These children! Why do they come here, day after day? Why do they serve us—and why don't they want any pay?"

The villagers looked at each other. "Why don't they want any pay?"

They were shaking their heads in confusion and concern, when suddenly the villagers heard a loud sneeze! "What was that?" cried Mayor Miser the Mad.

"It wasn't the dragon, that's for sure," The Baker Moocha More-eh said slowly.

"Then who was it!" demanded Auntie Ambition nervously.

"It was me!" Just Bad announced. He crawled out from

under the tablecloth, wiping his eyes. The Greed children all crawled out from their hiding places one by one...and the villagers were amazed.

"What are you doing here!" yelled Just Mad.

"What have you got to say for yourselves?" asked the mayor.

"I need a tissue!" declared Just Bad.

His mother handed him a tissue. "Now answer my question! What are you doing here?"

Just Bad blew his nose. "We *like* the kids who have been coming to our village!"

Stingy stood beside her brother and said, "These children have brought us laughter; these children have brought us joy!"

"These children have taught us manners!" Persnickety said with a bow.

"We've even been sharing our toys!" Just Bad said proudly.

"Sharing your toys?" The villagers echoed in dismay. Sharing anything was absolutely unheard of in the Village Greed. Mayor Miser the Mad was terribly embarrassed by his children. His wife was, of course, Just Mad. Fanciful and Ambition fanned themselves dramatically and then fainted.

Dark, Dingy, and Dirty stepped forward and quietly set a string of pearls and a gold watch on the table in front of the mayor and his wife. Mayor Miser the Mad and Just Mad gasped and screamed happily, "My gold watch!" "My pearls!"

"My goodness!" Smudge exclaimed at the unusual behavior of his three children.

"And they've taught us some beautiful songs!" Stingy declared. "They say there's a King who loves us!"

The villagers gasped in shock at such a statement. Ambition and Fanciful had been just getting back up off the floor, but at this, they fainted once again. The baker's daughter stood beside her mother. "What's love, Mother?"

"What's love?" Mucha More-eh echoed. "What's love? Why, I suppose it's the very thing I've been wanting *more* of all these years!" and she reached out to hug her little girl.

"They say there's a King who cares," Stingy continued.

"What do *you* care about, Daddy?" Just Bad asked Mayor Miser the Mad, but the mayor couldn't answer. Instead, he pulled his three children close and began to cry.

"The King sounds wonderful!" Persnickety said. "We must leave our Village of Greed!

The villagers looked at their children in dismay. "Leave Greed?" echoed Mayor Miser the Mad. "But our village has a name to uphold! A reputation have we! For miles around...our fame is renowned! We're known...as the People...Greed."

Instead of their usual pride in that fact, the villagers suddenly felt embarrassed. "We're known...as the People...Greed..." they repeated softly.

"Please!" said the children to their parents. "Let's leave Greed!"

For a few moments there was silence, then Smudge Yukerty said, "Perhaps an investigation would be in order to find out the reason why these children have crossed our borders! Why? Why? Why?"

The Greed villagers nodded their agreement, "Why do they come here, day after day? Why do they serve us? Why don't they want any pay?"

Mayor Miser the Mad pounded the table with great authority. He cleared his throat and spoke with his most dramatic voice. "Meeting adjourned! We will meet the children..."

At that very moment, there was another kind of pounding... actually it was a knocking. The villagers looked at each other in surprise. Just Mad went to open the door. There in the entrance stood the children from the Kingdom.

Chapter Seven

"Hello!" Seeker said. "We're sorry to bother you! We just wanted to let you know we're leaving now. We'll see you all again tomorrow." Seeker and his friends turned to go, but the mayor stopped them.

"Wait! Don't go!" The Kingdom children turned back questioningly. The mayor cleared his throat and spoke with his most dramatic voice, "Uh...we of the Village Greed have a question to ask you..."

The villagers nodded and stepped forward together. "Why do you come here day after day? Why do you serve us? Why don't you want any pay, no way? Why don't you want any pay?!"

Seeker and his friends smiled. "We come because the King sent us," Seeker answered. "He really loves you."

The villagers leaned forward with interest. "He does?"

"Yes!" said Seeker. "He *really* loves you!"

The mayor cleared his throat again. "Well, in the past, we have heard rumors about this King—how he makes his people give up everything—he doesn't let them have anything!"

"Oh no!" Seeker cried. "The King's not like that at all; he's wonderful!"

"Like you kids?" asked Just Bad.

Seeker was embarrassed by the little boy's compliment. "No, the King is much, much better than us!"

"Yes, he is always giving and giving!" Yes nodded.

HopeSo and KnowSo stepped forward and spoke to the mayor. "The King sent us here with a very important message for you!"

The children sang the King's message, and the people listened closely. The villagers knew that they needed to change...and here was the answer, the amazing answer. There was a King—a King who loved them and wanted to give them a new life!

There is a King who loves you;
There is a King who cares
There is a King who loves you—
A King who gives and shares.
He wants to give you new life in his Kingdom;
He wants to give you his joy and his peace.
He will fill your hearts with happiness and laughter
When you really get to know him!

During the song, the people of Greed began to cry—softly at first and then in loud wails. Just Mad and Mrs. Yukerty, who had been enemies for years, held each other and sobbed. "I'm so sorry for all the things we took that belonged to you!" Mrs. Yukerty cried.

"And I'm so sorry I didn't think to share them with you!" cried Just Mad. "I've spent so much time being mad, just mad!" Smudge passed out tissues, giving several handfuls to the mayor, who seemed to be crying even more loudly than everyone else.

The baker and his wife hugged Fanciful and Auntie Ambition. "We've been so busy trying to fill the emptiness inside that we never took time to care for other people!" Moocha More-eh said, crying.

Auntie Ambition and Fanciful responded tearfully, "And we told lies to you about how full and happy we were! But we weren't full; we've been empty, so empty!"

When the children finished singing, Mayor Miser the Mad blew his nose a final time and cleared his throat, "Well, I believe I speak for all of us (the villagers nodded their agreement); we're tired of being greedy! It seems we've always had what we thought we wanted, but never got what we *really* wanted...if you see what I mean..."

"I've always dreamed of being happy," cried Fanciful, "but I've never *been happy*."

"I've wasted so many years," wept Auntie Ambition, "dreaming and scheming."

Mrs. Yukerty stepped forward. "But we didn't really know there was a better way...until you children came here and told us!"

"Until you children came here and showed us!" Smudge Yukerty exclaimed. "Now we know *why* you've come here every day—it's because of *him!*"

"Because of *him!*" Seeker nodded excitedly. "Because he *loves* you. He wants you to have a brand new life in his Kingdom! He wants you to get to *know* him."

The mayor cleared his throat loudly. "Well, I believe I speak for all of us (the villagers again nodded their agreement); we want to...we need to...get to know the King."

"Hooray! Hooray!" The Kingdom children cheered, then remembered something very important. "Oh, just a minute! Do you really want to know the King?"

"Uh-huh!" the villagers responded.

The children shook their heads and folded their arms firmly. "Uh-uh!! Do you *really* want to know the King?"

"Yes!" the villagers responded with great enthusiasm. "We *really* want to know the King!"

"Then you *shall* know the King!"

To the absolute surprise of everyone, the King himself stepped out from a place near the village where he had been waiting to be found.

"The *King!*" The Kingdom children crowded around to greet the King, while the people of Greed watched with shy astonishment. It was really true. There truly was a King! And here, all those years, they had believed a lie. They had believed a lot of lies.

The villagers rubbed their eyes and looked again at the King, when suddenly, from beside the gate came a terrible ROAR!

The dragon Greed summoned his last remaining strength and rushed toward the crowd. The people screamed and immediately fell back. The villagers held their children closely and trembled with fear.

The dragon was definitely smaller than he had been. His strength had slowly been destroyed by the children's giving, and he was now so small that his clothing sagged around his frail body. But the dragon's anger had not grown smaller; it had grown very, very big. He rushed toward the King with hatred streaming from his face. His breath came in disgusting green smelly gasps. "They are under my control!" he screamed in a slobbering rage. "I'm the one who feeds them!"

"They belong to you no more!" said the King with calm authority. "This day I've come to free them! Loving to give, not loving to get; singing, and sharing, Greed...to forget!"

The King folded his arms and stood tall and strong in all of his majestic royal power. Then the King lifted his voice and began to sing.

> *I have come to seek and save the lost;*
> *I bought freedom at a very high cost!*
> *When they call to me I always come,*
> *And I command the Darkness,*
> *I command the Darkness—*
> *To be gone!*

It was an incredible song. The King's words and music sent the walls of the Village Greed tumbling to the ground. The dragon writhed in pain. He circled the King, roaring and whining and crying...and shrinking even smaller than he already was!

Then the King laughed. He laughed and laughed and laughed. Then he laughed some more, until, with one final angry roar, the dragon disappeared. (It returned to its wicked master in the deep dark place beneath the trap door of the CARNALville of Selfishness. From there, sadly, it would likely be sent to work at other villages beyond the mountains.)

After a few unbelieving moments, the villagers whispered in amazement, "It's gone! The dragon is gone!" The village children jumped up and down and cried, "Hooray for the King! Hooray for the King!"

The King looked at his army of children, leaned forward, and winked. "Fine work, everyone! A little bit of giving can overcome a whole lot of greed!" the children smiled back at him happily.

"Well, King," Seeker said, "I guess we'd better introduce you to everyone!"

"Yes, Seeker," nodded the King. "I want to give each person a new name!"

Do took hold of the King's hand and lead him over to the mayor, who was nervously bowing his head. "This is the mayor!" Do said.

The mayor continued to bow his head. He spoke softly, embarrassed at who they had been. "Yes, uh, Your Majesty, I'm Mayor Miser the Mad. My wife here, she's Just Mad, and our three children are Stingy, Persnickety, and Just Bad."

The King reached out to welcome the mayor and his family into his Kingdom. "From now on you shall be Mayor Giving and Glad! Your wife shall be Just Glad, and your children shall be Sharing, Fairness, and...and you," the King said as he knelt down to look Just Bad in the eye, "you shall be called, Just Good! Do you think that you can live up to that name, son?"

Just Good smiled and said, "Yes sir. If you *really* help me!"

"I will help you!" the King said, standing to his feet.

Yes took his hand next and introduced the baker's family. "This is the Baker Moocha More-eh, and his wife, Mucha More-eh, and their daughter, Megga More-eh!"

The baker was holding his family and blowing his nose loudly. "Excuse me, sir, it's just that we've always wanted *more*, but nothing ever filled up the emptiness..."

"Until now!" the baker's daughter, Megga, cried out and threw her arms around the King.

The King picked the little girl up in his great arms and twirled her around. His laughter filled the air and swept through the streets of the village, removing even more traces of what had always been. The King's laughter burst into the hearts of the people, and for the first time in their lives, they felt happy and full.

The King touched the baker and his family, saying, "You are the Baker Bounti*full*; your wife is *Full*fillment, and your daughter is Joy*full!*"

Giggles led the King over to Auntie Ambition and Fanciful, who were fanning themselves nervously. "You will find the happiness you have dreamed of in my Kingdom," the King declared, "and your names will be Hope and Destiny!" The ladies smiled radiantly at the King and curtsied.

"This is Smudge Yukerty," Gladness announced.

"Hello, Your Majesty," Smudge bowed low. "Meet my wife, Mrs. Yukerty, and our three children, Dark, Dingy, and Dirty." Smudge reached out to shake the King's hand, then suddenly realized how dirty he felt...how dirty he *was*. He tried to wipe his hands off, but they just looked worse. He stood, very embarrassed, in front of the King. Then to Smudge's complete surprise, the King reached out and hugged him close!

"From now on," the King said with a sparkle in his eyes, "You shall be Smudge Cleaner!" And instantly, Smudge and his family were sparkling clean!

"Oh!" cried Smudge. "I'm Smudge Cleaner now!"

"Mrs. Cleaner," the King smiled, kissing her hand, "and your children are Bright, Neat, and Tidy!" Mrs. Cleaner giggled shyly and hugged her family close.

"And now," the King said to the villagers, "I will tell you about your new home in my Kingdom!"

"Where is our new home, King?" asked the village children.

"It is called the Village of Generosity!" The King smiled a mysterious smile. "It's not far away; no, in fact, it is very, very close!"

The King began to tell the people all about their new home. And he told them in a song. The villagers hugged each other and wept and danced as the King sang.

In the Village of Generosity—
You will live in the
Kingdom of Joy and Peace;
I have prepared a place especially for you
And you, and you, and you!
I will take away your selfish hearts;
I will give you lots of loving thoughts,
All your anxious worries—they will cease
I give you peace...
I will pour my love inside of you;
Clean hearts you'll have inside of you;
You won't love to get —
You'll love to give!

Something wonderful happened as the villagers hugged each other and wept and danced and sang with the King. The Village Greed melted away, and in its place, the Village of Generosity sparkled in the sunlight. Certain parts of the old village remained. Certain parts like the carefully weeded flowerbeds, the freshly mowed lawns, and the newly painted doors. The King had used every gift that the children of the Kingdom had given—every helpful and kind thing they had done—to help build a new home for the villagers.

"Thank you, King! Thank you, children! Thank you for rescuing us from the dragon!" the villagers cried.

The villagers turned toward Generosity and made excited happy comments as they entered the gate. "Oh, it's wonderful!" "It's even better than wonderful—it's magnificent!" "It's more than anything I could ever have imagined!" "It's absolutely beautiful!" "It's absolutely home."

Seeker and his friends watched the people of Generosity go into their new homes. Then the children walked with the King back to Peace and Harmony. Giggles took one of the King's hands and asked, "Anybody want to play another game of hide and seek when we get back to the castle?" Everyone laughed.

The next week at the King's Celebration, the third banqueting table was filled with the happy, laughing people from the Village of Generosity. The King looked over at Seeker and his friends, leaned forward, and winked. The children quickly got up from their places at the banquet tables and ran up to the throne.

"Look, King!" Seeker said happily, "your banquet is full!"

The King didn't answer. The children looked at each other in surprise. The King still didn't speak; he just smiled one of his most mysterious smiles. Something about the way the King's eyes twinkled, and something about his mysterious smile, made Seeker and his friends realize that their adventures in his Kingdom had only just begun.

Think About the Story

Like the first story, this story is also true. There truly is a King and a Kingdom...and there truly is a dragon Greed. Every person must choose whether they will live in the Kingdom or whether they will live a selfish life filled with greed. Where will *you* live?

Talk to the King

"King Jesus, I don't want to live in the Village Greed, always wanting more, but never feeling full and happy inside. I want to live in Your Kingdom like Seeker and his friends. I want to be part of Your army. I want to destroy the power of greed by giving and serving and helping. I want my life to be an adventure!"

Read from the King's Great Book—Romans 12:21

Don't be overcome by evil!
Overcome evil with good!
Romans 12:21 uh-huh, uh-huh;
Romans 12:21 uh-huh, uh-huh;
(Great Book Paraphrase)

Part Three

Secret of
the Blue Pouch

Introduction

Lurking in the shadows somewhere between the CARNAL-ville of Selfishness and the Kingdom of Joy and Peace was a dragon.

He appeared to be small and unimportant; but this dragon was actually more evil and more cunning than many other dragons.

As he sneaked through bushes and trees, the dragon was singing his life-song, *"I have worked so hard, and I deserve the best; it's only fair and right—that I have more, not less...."*

The dragon's name was Itsalmine.

Earlier that day, Itsalmine had met with the dragon-clowns and their master in the deep dark place beneath the trap door of the CARNALville of Selfishness. It was agreed that he would be the perfect dragon to send on a very important assignment. His job was to sneak into the Kingdom of Joy and Peace and turn the children back to their former lives at the CARNALville. One particular child was the target.

"The child known as Seeker," the dragon-clowns had spoken to Itsalmine in low voices. "Find something...anything...and make him want it more than he wants the King. The other children will soon follow him back here to Selfishness."

Now, in the early morning shadows, Itsalmine crept toward Seeker's home in the Village of Peace and Harmony near the castle. As he neared the Kingdom borders, Itsalmine considered his plan.

I will find something that is already important to the boy, he thought, something that he wants very much. Then, all I have to do is make him want it more!

The nasty little dragon rubbed his claws together in anticipation, picked his nose thoughtfully, and laughed a quiet but very wicked laugh.

Chapter One

Seeker emptied the coins onto his bed and counted them one more time.

Fifteen! He almost had enough! Seeker carefully put the coins back into his money pouch. It was a special money pouch. He had made it himself from soft blue leather with a red drawstring. There was no other pouch like it in the world. Seeker clutched it tightly to his chest. Just one more coin and he would finally have the right amount!

Seeker wanted a bow and a quiver full of arrows with blue and red feathers on the ends. He knew exactly which set he wanted because he had cut a picture out of a catalog. It cost sixteen coins. He kept the picture in the top drawer of his dresser in a special little white box.

Seeker loved to look at the picture of the bow and arrow set and then run around his room, shooting invisible dragons and singing a song he had made up:

Hit the bull's-eye!
I will be a mighty warrior
With my trusty bow and arrows
I will run with might toward the foe—oh—
Dragons to the left and dragons to the right
I won't be afraid to fight

I'll lift my bow and arrow in the air—there!
Hit the bull's-eye!

For many months, Seeker had been saving money. He had worked at odd jobs around the Village of Peace and Harmony, and sold pictures that he had drawn of his adventures in the Kingdom. The coins earned from all his hard work, plus a few coins he had received for his birthday, were kept safely in the blue leather pouch and hidden underneath his mattress.

No one, absolutely no one, knew about the fifteen coins. The money in the blue leather pouch was a secret, and Seeker hadn't told any of his friends or anyone in his family. His mother thought he spent all of his money. Seeker had asked and asked her to buy a bow and arrow set for him, but her answer was always the same, "When you are older, Seeker, then you can have a bow and arrow set. Perhaps someday you could even earn the money to buy it yourself."

And I *did* earn the money myself! Seeker thought happily. Only one more coin to go! I just need sixteen coins to buy the best bow and quiver of arrows in the village! And then I can surprise everybody! Soon I will be a mighty warrior for the King!

Thinking again about the catalog picture, Seeker lifted up an imaginary bow, set an imaginary arrow in it, and then let it fly. I'll lift my bow and arrow in the air—there! Hit the bull's-eye!

Seeker didn't realize it, but a nasty little dragon had watched him count the coins. He didn't realize that the nasty little dragon, Itsalmine, was now rubbing his claws together in delight and breathing selfish thoughts into Seeker's mind: *All yours. Every coin is all yours.*

"It's all mine," Seeker smiled happily. "Every coin is all mine."

You worked hard. You saved your money and you deserve every single coin.

"I worked hard. I saved my money, and I deserve every single coin..."

You can get whatever you want...it's only fair and right...

"I can get whatever I want...it's only fair and right..."

And you deserve the very best!

"And I deserve the very best!"

The best bow and arrow set in the village!

"The best bow and arrow set in the village!"

Itsalmine moved closer and began to sing into Seeker's mind, *You have worked so hard, and you deserve the best; it's only fair and right—that you have more, not less....*

Seeker hummed and rocked back and forth, clutching the blue leather pouch to his chest dreamily. "I have worked so hard, and I deserve the best; it's only fair and right—that I have more, not less...." Seeker had no idea that a dragon hummed along with him and that the dragon had grown a little bit bigger than he had been before...

"Seeker!" his mother's voice interrupted his thoughts. "Weren't you planning to meet your friends at the Big Rock by now?"

"Oh yeah! Thanks, Mom!"

Seeker and his friends were planning to meet at the rock near the base of the Straight and Narrow Path. Then they were going to the castle to spend time with the King. Quickly hiding the blue leather pouch beneath his mattress, Seeker ran out of the house, raced through the streets of Peace and Harmony, and came to a skidding halt at the foot of the Straight and Narrow Path.

Chapter Two

"**S**orry I'm late!" Seeker called to his friends, but they didn't answer him. HopeSo, KnowSo, and Yes; Giggles, Gladness, and Glee; and Dawdle and Slow were all gathered around Doodle and Do. Everyone looked worried. Seeker moved in closer to hear what they were saying.

"Please!" KnowSo exclaimed, "Tell us what's wrong! We want to *know*!"

"You tell them, Doodle," said Do.

"No, you do it, Do!" responded Doodle.

"C'mon, Doodle! Do it!" insisted Do.

"Oh, all right," Doodle agreed with a sigh. "I'll *do* it."

Doodle turned to their friends. "It's our big brother, Daring. He's been in the King's service across the sea, and it's been months and months since we've seen him! Now he's close to home—his ship is anchored along the coast about twenty miles north of Royal Harbor. He's only going to be there for a few days, and we *really* want to go see him; but we can't!"

"Why can't you?" asked the children. This time, Do answered. "Well, Mom and Dad are going to go tomorrow, but we don't have enough money for all of us to go," he said sadly. "This morning Mom told us that we need at least another fifteen coins to pay for all of us to travel and stay overnight..."

"Fifteen coins!" Seeker echoed in surprise.

The dragon Itsalmine had been hiding quietly, but now quickly moved close to Seeker. *Yours! The coins are yours! You don't have to give them up!* he breathed.

"Mine," Seeker whispered to himself. "The money is mine... It's all mine. I have worked so hard, and I deserve the best; it's only fair and right—that I have more, not less...!"

The words raced through his mind while the other children discussed possible solutions for Doodle and Do's problem.

Then KnowSo exclaimed, "I *know!* Let's go and talk to the King about Doodle and Do's problem! He will *know* what to do!"

"Yes!" everyone agreed. "The King will know what to do!" And off they ran up the Straight and Narrow Path toward the castle; but Seeker didn't run. He walked, slowly and thoughtfully, not realizing that he was listening to the voice of a dragon.

"I have worked so hard, and I deserve the best; it's only fair and right—that I have more, not less...."

When Seeker reached the door of the castle, Itsalmine hid behind a tree, happily realizing that he had grown again. Now he was a little larger and a little stronger than he had been. He stood picking his nose.

"Dragons aren't allowed within the castle walls," he mumbled to himself, "Unless, of course...unless someone happens to open a door!"

He laughed a wicked little laugh and waited.

Chapter Three

When the children arrived at the castle courtyard, the King was there to meet them.

"King!" they cried, "Doodle and Do have a problem!"

"I *know*," responded the King.

"They need fifteen coins so they can go see their brother," explained HopeSo.

"I *know*," the King said again.

The King put his great arms around Doodle and Do's shoulders and bent down on one knee to look into their eyes. "Do you trust me?" he asked the young boys. When they nodded a determined *yes*, the King said, "Will you continue to trust me, even if your problem is very, very big?" he asked quietly.

The other children had been watching. They smiled at each other. No problem was too big for the King!

"We'll trust you, King!" said Doodle.

Do nodded. "Even if our very big problem is called fifteen coins, we'll trust you, King!"

The boys looked at each other, smiled and spoke together, "It's what we're going to *do!*"

The King laughed and hugged them close. Then he stood up, turned to the other children, and said, "Come on everybody; today I want to take you to one of my favorite places!"

The children cheered and grabbed hold of the King's hands. "Wh-wh-where are we g-g-going, King?" asked Dawdle.

"A-a-are we g-g-going on an adventure, King?" asked Slow.

The children loved going on adventures in the Kingdom. "Are we going to fight some dragons today, King?" Seeker asked excitedly. He was remembering how they had rescued people of Greed from the dragon.

The King smiled a mysterious smile. "There are many kinds of dragons, Seeker. And some of the greatest battles are fought right in here." The King gently touched Seeker's heart. The King's touch was hot, so hot that Seeker pulled away in surprise. An uncomfortable knot formed in his stomach, and he couldn't look at the King's eyes.

The other children tugged at the King, "Let's get going to your favorite place!" Glee said. "Where is it?"

The King laughed. "It's just down that walkway over there. Do you see that hall that's extra shiny?"

Giggles laughed. "Extra shiny means extra slippery!"

The King laughed, too, and took his shoes off. "I'll race you!" he called; and off they went.

Usually Seeker was one of the best at sliding down the shining Kingdom halls and walkways, but today he didn't feel like sliding or playing. He felt like thinking about his money.

Fifteen coins...So what if Doodle and Do need fifteen coins, and I just happen to have fifteen coins?! The King will look after Doodle and Do. It's not my problem.

The very moment when Seeker decided to think like that, a door someplace in the castle wall was opened. It was just the right size for the wicked dragon, Itsalmine, to squeeze through. He immediately began to breathe thoughts in Seeker's direction....

I worked hard for my money, and it's all mine, Seeker thought. *It's all mine! And I can spend it on whatever I want...*

I have worked so hard, and I deserve the best; it's only fair and right—that I have more, not less....

Seeker walked slowly. Thoughts of the CARNALville of Selfishness, where he and the other children used to spend many of their days, began to form in his mind. Seeker hadn't thought about that place for a long time. *I could even use my money to play at the CARNALville*, Seeker thought to himself, *It wasn't such a bad place. The candy sure was good...Yeah...The special secret recipe candy....It sure was good...*

The dragon Itsalmine came even closer, growing a bit larger with each step. Seeker said aloud, "Maybe I should forget about the bow and arrow set for a while and go visit the CARNALville. That stuff about being a mighty warrior was dumb anyway. I could never be a mighty warrior...I could never really hit the bull's-eye." Seeker licked his lips dreamily. "Hmm...I sure could go for just one little piece of that CARNALville candy...I haven't had any for so long..."

"Seeker! What are you *do*ing?" Doodle yelled as he came running toward his friend. "Hurry! The King is going to take us inside the White Tower! Hurry!"

"The White Tower?" Seeker echoed. "Uh..."

The dragon Itsalmine pulled, unseen, at Seeker's arm, whispering and drooling, "CARNALville candy...yummy, yummy CARNALville candy..."

"Uh..." Seeker said again.

"What's wrong with you, Seeker?" asked Doodle. "You know how much we've been wanting to get into that tower!"

The White Tower in the far corner of the castle gardens had been especially interesting to the children because it was locked. Every other place in the Kingdom was open to them, but each time they had tried to turn the handle on that one little tower, it refused to turn.

"Hurry, Seeker!" Doodle said again. "Come on!"

"Uh...Uh...OK, I guess so." Seeker turned to go with his friend. The dragon tried to reach out his foot and trip Seeker, but it didn't work. (Dragon powers are very limited inside the castle walls.) Itsalmine stomped his feet and pouted. *Oh, well. Seeker would have to wait. He had something else he needed to do right now anyway...*

Chapter Four

At the White Tower, Seeker and his friends looked with great surprise at the wooden door. Some letters had appeared right in the center of it!

> I am the Tower of Knowledge
> Great desire is my key
> If you *really* want to
> You can get my key from the King

The children turned excitedly to the King. "Is this your favorite place, King?" asked Gladness.

The King nodded. *"One* of my favorites!"

"Do we get to go inside?" asked Doodle.

"Do you have the key? Do you? Do you, King?" Do and the others tugged at the King's hands.

"A key? Let's see, it should be here somewhere." The King smiled mysteriously and searched through his pockets.

The children waited patiently, and the King realized that he needed to give them a hint. "The key is actually the answer to my favorite question!" He folded his arms, leaned forward, and winked. "Do you *really* want to go in there?"

The children laughed. Of course! Here in the Kingdom, the only way you got into places was by *really* wanting to! They all said together, "Yes! We *really* want to!"

Immediately, the King pulled a beautiful golden key from his pocket. Then, very slowly, he put the key into the lock, turned it, and the door swung open.

The children looked around with big eyes, their mouths open in amazement. There were doors and stairways, doors and stairways, and more doors and more stairways—hundreds and hundreds of doors and stairways! "Wow..." Seeker whispered, "how can all of this fit into one little tower?!"

KnowSo was very impressed. "Now I *know* why this is one of your favorite places, King!" he said.

The children quickly began to explore. They ran up flights of stairs and then slid down the banisters, winding their way through each level. They slid down the shining hallways, across great balconies, and past countless doorways.

Above each door was a sign. Most of the words were difficult for the children to read. Many were blurry. Doodle and Do had been busily climbing to the highest level in the tower. They read the sign above the highest door. "King!" they called down to him. "We just read the sign above this door. It says, 'Doorway to My Father's Kingdom.' What does that mean?"

The King laughed and called out, "It means 'Doorway to My Father's Kingdom!'"

"King!" Doodle cried, *"Do* you have a dad?"

"Can we see him, King, can we?"

"Someday, when it is time, I will take you there myself to meet him. But right now, I want you all to come close to me. I have something special to show you."

Doodle and Do slid together down a series of banisters, talking excitedly. "The King is even better than I always thought he was!" said Doodle.

Do agreed, "He's amazing! Just think—all this inside one little tower!"

Doodle leaned over and whispered to his brother, *"Do* you think the King can fix our big problem with one little answer?"

Do giggled, "Yes, I *do!*"

In the center of the Tower of Knowledge, on a glistening

cabinet, was a book trimmed with gold. Light was shining out from its pages. As the children crowded around, the King said, "This is my book...the Great Book." The children peered into the pages and read aloud, "'Thee, thou, hitherto, wherefore'"...Glee shook her head, looked up, and said, "King, we don't understand these big words!"

The King smiled another of his mysterious smiles and answered, "Then I will open your eyes so that you can!" He stretched out his great hands and gently touched the children's eyes. When they looked again at the Great Book, they could understand the words. The King held the book open for them as they read page after page...

Seeker pointed at the first page excitedly. "Look! This is where the world came from!"

"Wow!" the other children said together.

"Yes!" Yes said, pointing at the next page. "This is where the birds came from, and the animals, and the people!"

"Wow!" the other children said together.

"Look at this!" cried HopeSo. "Look at all these stories! This is about a flood and a big, big boat!"

The King continued opening the pages and the children continued with their excited comments. "Look what this person did...look what this person did...ooh, look what that person did!"

They looked farther and farther through the pages of the book. Then Seeker pointed and said, "King, here are some words I don't understand. It says, 'Whoever saves his life, will lose it...and whoever loses his life will find it.' What does it mean—if you find your life you lose it; and if you lose your life, you find it?"

The King's eyes twinkled. "Would you like me to tell you what the words mean, or *show* you what the words mean? My messenger will take you..."

Just then, HopeSo pointed at the book and cried out, "Look, King! The book talks about a man who sounds just like you!"

Everyone forgot about Seeker's question as the King answered HopeSo. *"Really?"* he asked with interest.

"Yes!" Yes nodded excitedly. "There are stories in here about a man who likes children and does great things and has a Kingdom!"

Giggles giggled. "He *does* sound just like you, King!"

"Really?" the King said again.

"B-b-but look what happened to the man!" Dawdle exclaimed.

"They wh-wh-whipped him...and did really m-m-mean things to him..." Slow said slowly.

"And then they put nails into his hands and feet...and he died!" HopeSo whispered.

Giggles sadly shook her head and whispered, "They took his life away."

Doodle was horrified. "Why did they *do* that? Why would they take his life away like that!"

Everyone was thoughtful and quiet, then the King spoke softly. "Perhaps they *didn't* take his life away."

The children looked up at the King. He was smiling the most mysterious smile they had ever seen. "Perhaps," he said even more softly, "Perhaps he *gave* his life...willingly."

A sense of wonder filled the children's hearts. "Why would he *do* something like that, King?" Do asked.

The King's smile deepened. "He would do it...He would give his life, because he knew it was the only way to open the door."

Seeker and his friends were puzzled. "Door? What door?"

The King looked up at the highest door in the Tower of Knowledge. "That door!"

Doodle and Do looked at each other, and then at the King. "Doorway to My Father's Kingdom?"

All of the children turned together and looked at the King. He met their eyes for a moment, then looked down. The children followed the King's gaze...down to his big hands that were holding open the pages of the Great Book. Two faded old scars were on his hands; so faded that the children had never noticed them before.

KnowSo gasped. "You are the man in the book!"

Seeker nodded, "They didn't take your life from you...you gave it up!"

The King laughed. It was a joyful laugh that came from deep inside himself. "Yes! I gave my life, and because I did, you can have life! Someday, when it is the right time, each of you who believes in me will go through the door to my father's Kingdom... and what awaits you there is far greater than anything that you have ever dreamed or imagined!"

Yes moved closer to the King. Her eyes filled up with tears as she gently took both of the King's hands in her own. She very tenderly stroked the old faded scars and then kissed them. "Thank you, King," she whispered. "Thank you for giving your life...for us."

The other children crowded in closer to the King, hugging him and gently patting his hands. "Thank you, King. Thank you." Love for the King filled their hearts. They had loved him before, but now they really loved him.

After many long moments, Seeker whispered, "Whoever saves his life, will lose it...and whoever loses his life will find it." He looked up at the King. "Those were the words I started to ask you about before. You were just about to explain...you said..."

The King's eyes twinkled. "I said, 'Would you like me to tell you what the words mean, or *show* you what the words mean?'"

Suddenly, on the other side of the Tower of Knowledge, a door burst open, and a Messenger came in. He was very, very old, but very, very young at the same time. He was dressed in a royal tunic and carried a scroll and a golden trumpet. He bowed deeply to the King and asked, "Now?"

"Now!" laughed the King. He turned to the children. "Go with my Messenger. He will show you what the words from the Great Book mean!"

The Messenger blew his golden trumpet and then sang:

> *Hear ye, hear ye, hear ye—*
> *A story from the book!*
> *Open your ears to hear it;*
> *Open up your eyes and look.*

The children happily joined in the Messenger's song and followed him...out the door through which he had just entered...

Chapter Five

Suddenly, the children were standing on a hill they had never seen before. Tall grasses waved in the wind and a blue lake sparkled at the base of the hill. The Tower of Knowledge had disappeared.

"Wh-wh-where are we?" Dawdle and Slow wondered.

"I've never seen this hill before...and I've never seen that lake, either," Yes said, standing closer to Seeker.

"Was the wind blowing today, KnowSo?" Seeker whispered.

"No, it wasn't," KnowSo whispered back.

"This is very peculiar!" Giggles giggled nervously.

"How can all this fit inside one little tower?" Glee asked the question that each of the children was wondering.

"I'd like to *know* how that door can just stand there by itself!" KnowSo said, looking back at the door they had come through and shaking his head in wonder. The other children looked at the door and shook their heads, too.

But there was no more time to wonder because the Messenger was still singing and leading them across the hill....

The children followed the Messenger until they reached a spot where they could look over the other side of the hill. There the Messenger stopped, put one finger to his lips to quiet the children, and then pointed. Coming toward them was a crowd of people.

The children sank down into the grass and watched as the crowd came closer. The people were dressed differently than they had ever seen before. There were lots of children skipping and playing as they climbed the hill, but a few of them had to be carried. Seeker and his friends noticed then that many of the people were sick or crippled; and they realized that the whole crowd was following one man.

"Look at that man!" Giggles pointed and whispered. "He looks just like the King! He..."

Gladness stopped his sister. "That man doesn't just *look* like the King..."

"That man *is* the King." The children whispered together in amazement. They turned their heads toward the Messenger who was smiling at them.

"What is this place?" KnowSo asked. "Where are we?"

"And who are you, anyway?" HopeSo asked.

"I am the King's Messenger!" He bowed slightly and smiled again. "When you *really* want to understand something from the Great Book, I will be there to bring it to life for you!"

KnowSo nodded, "I get it—when we *really* wanted to know what it means to 'lose your life and find it'..."

The Messenger smiled and said, "The King told me to bring you here...inside this story from the Great Book. Now, open up your eyes...and look." He pointed back toward the people and the Man on the hill.

They all watched silently as the Man took some children from the crowd up onto his knees and hugged them. The children that were being carried were laid down at his feet. Seeker and his friends watched in wonder as the Man reached out and touched those children, and within moments they stood up, totally well!

"Wow!" Seeker and the others whispered.

Then someone brought a blind man to the man, and he healed the blind man so he could see. He healed the cripples so they could walk, and he healed the sick people so they were well. Every person the man touched was very, very happy. The whole crowd began to cheer and jump up and down and hug each other.

Then, in the midst of all that happiness, a young man wearing rich-looking clothes and shining jewels rode up the hill on a camel. Servants helped him get onto the ground and then bowed low as he passed them and pushed his way through the crowd. He stood proudly in front of the man on the hill.

"Oooh..." said Giggles, giggling. "He sure must be somebody important!"

Glee nodded, "Or at least, he *thinks* he is somebody important!"

"I'm sure *glad* I don't have to get around on a camel!" Gladness said, holding his nose.

Suddenly, Do pointed, "Yuck! *Do* you see it?"

"See what?" the others asked.

"*Do* you see the dragon?"

"Dragon?!" the other children sat up taller and strained to see.

"I see it," Giggles said, not giggling. "There—right behind that rich guy! Oh yuck! It's picking its nose!"

"That is so disgusting!" Yes cried, moving closer to Seeker.

Hiding very closely behind the rich man, so closely that he could hardly be seen, was the wicked little dragon, Itsalmine. Except now, he was not little...he was enormous! The rich man had been feeding the selfish dragon for many years.

"Good master," the rich man spoke loudly to the Man on the hill, "what must I do to have eternal life?"

The Man replied, "If you want to have eternal life, give up what you have to the poor and come and follow me!"

"Give up what you have?" The dragon Itsalmine was so startled that he nearly stepped out from his hiding place. The dragon and the rich man shook their heads together stubbornly.

Then, the rich young man reached inside his cloak, searching for something. Seeker watched—and gasped! From inside his cloak the rich young man pulled out...a little blue leather pouch tied with a red drawstring! Seeker couldn't believe his eyes! He leapt to his feet and yelled out, "Hey! How did you get that? That's my blue leather pouch! Where did you..."

Seeker couldn't finish the sentence because the other children pulled him back to the ground. "Shh! Sit down, Seeker!"

"Wh-Wh-What's the m-ma-matter, Seeker?" asked Dawdle.

"A-A-Are you OK?" Slow asked, concerned.

"That guy has my blue leather pouch! I made it myself! No one else could have one just like it!" Seeker struggled to get up again, and then realized the Messenger was motioning for them to watch the scene before them.

The rich young man was still holding up the blue leather pouch. Suddenly the dragon leaned into him even more closely and spoke with convincing power, "You have worked so hard, and you deserve the best; it's only fair and right—that you have more, not less...."

The rich man echoed the dragon's words, "I have worked so hard, and I deserve the best; it's only fair and right—that I have more, not less...."

Seeker turned very pale. "Those words," he whispered to himself. "Those words. I thought those exact words this morning after I counted my coins! And I've been singing those exact words all day long!"

Seeker watched as the rich young man held the blue leather pouch to his chest with one hand and patted the dragon with the other, his eyes never leaving the Man's. Moments passed and the children hardly breathed. What would happen? Would he do what the Man asked?

"Oh, I get it!" KnowSo whispered. "Whosoever saves his life, will lose it...and whoever loses his life will find it!"

The other children turned questioningly. "What?"

"That's why we're here!" KnowSo whispered excitedly, "The Messenger brought us here so we would really understand what those words mean! Don't you get it?"

The children nodded and HopeSo said, "Yeah, I get it! I understand, and I sure hope that rich guy does!"

"Come on, rich guy!" Giggles whispered earnestly. "Make the right choice!"

Everyone joined Giggles in her whispered cheer. "Come on, rich guy! You can do it! Come on! Make the right choice! Give it up!"

More moments passed. Then the rich young man cleared his throat. The children held their breath, but to their great disappointment, the rich man firmly and stubbornly shook his head. "It's all mine," he said, "and I can't give it up...not even for you." Then he turned and walked away.

And the Man on the hill looked very, very sad.

Then the whole scene vanished. The crowd was gone, the rich man was gone, even the camel was gone. The children looked around, wondering, but nothing remained except the wind-blown grass on the hill. Then, to their amazement, the King was sitting in front of them on the hill...looking right at Seeker. The intense way that the King looked at him made Seeker feel uncomfortable, and he turned away. The knot inside his stomach had returned, now even tighter than before.

"I understand, King," KnowSo said as he ran to sit next to the King. "The words in the Great Book—'Whoever saves his life, will lose it...and whoever loses his life will find it.'"

"Yes!" nodded Yes with excitement. "The rich young man wanted his money more than he wanted you, King!"

Gladness agreed. "So instead of really finding life, he lost it. Wow. That was a great story; but I sure don't feel *glad* about the choice that rich guy made!"

"*Do* you think we can go back into the Tower now, King?" asked Doodle. "I want to look at that Great Book again!"

The King nodded toward the Messenger, who led them back to the door that was still standing on the other side of the hill. The Messenger smiled and waved good-bye as the children stepped through the doorway with the King. Immediately, they were back inside the Tower of Knowledge.

Chapter Six

"**I** have a gift for you," the King said as he walked over to the glistening cabinet in the center of the Tower of Knowledge. The King opened a drawer and took out miniature copies of the Great Book. Every copy looked just like the Great Book, but smaller—so the children could actually carry the Book with them! The King gave one to each of the children. "Read from this Book every day," he said. "In it are the laws, the promises, the treasures of my Kingdom. Through its pages, you will get to know me better."

The King handed HopeSo and KnowSo their copies and said, "Look inside right now. You will see a bookmark to help you remember what you learned today..."

"Here are those words again," KnowSo said, "'Whoever saves his life, will lose it...and whoever loses his life will find it!'"

"Wow," the children said, carefully flipping through the pages. "This is so awesome!"

When the King gave a copy of the Great Book to Doodle and Do, he said, "As you read my Book, you will realize that no problem is too big, even if it is a very, very big problem. You will learn to trust me."

"We will really trust you, King!" said Doodle.

Do nodded. "Even if our very big problem is called fifteen coins, we'll trust you!" The boys looked at each other, smiled, and spoke together, "It's what we're going to *do!*"

Seeker was watching. He watched as the King hugged Doodle and Do closely. Fifteen coins, Seeker thought again. *They need fifteen coins. I have fifteen coins in my blue leather pouch...at least, I thought I did. Maybe that rich guy in the story got into my room somehow and took my pouch! How could he have one exactly like it?*

At that very moment, the King turned toward Seeker, smiled, and handed him a copy of the Great Book. "Reading my book will help you to make good choices and wise decisions, Seeker. It will help you to become a mighty warrior for me."

"Mighty warrior?" Seeker looked up, surprised. Then, he turned away and shook his head. "Not me, King. I'll never be a mighty warrior."

The King put his hand on the boy's shoulder, but Seeker refused to look up. He was embarrassed to realize that his eyes had begun to fill with tears. He mumbled a *thank you* as he stuffed the book into his backpack and ran out of the Tower of Knowledge.

Seeker ran all the way down the Straight and Narrow Path, through the Village of Peace and Harmony, into his house, up the stairs, and into his bedroom. Frantically, he reached under his mattress and pulled out the blue leather pouch.

"It's still here! It wasn't my pouch that rich guy had after all! But, it was the same color, the same shape—I made this myself! No one could have one exactly like it!"

He opened the pouch and shook out the fifteen coins, quickly counting them. "One, two, three...fifteen! Whew! Every single coin is still here!"

Very carefully, Seeker inspected the blue leather pouch. "I don't understand! How could that guy have exactly the same pouch as me? I don't get it!"

He sat on his bed with a sigh. "Hmm...the King sure looked sad when that rich man wouldn't give it up and follow him. And the King sure looked sad at me when he sat on the hill. The King couldn't know about my fifteen coins...or could he? And if he does know...does he think I'm acting like that rich guy?" Seeker shivered. "What a scary thought!"

Other thoughts raced through Seeker's mind as he gathered the coins up and put them back inside the pouch.

"Doodle and Do really need fifteen coins. I want Doodle and Do to be happy; I want them to see their brother. But I really want a bow and arrow! I want to be a mighty warrior!" Thinking again about the catalog picture, Seeker lifted up an imaginary bow, but this time he lifted it more slowly than usual. Then he set an imaginary arrow in the bow, and let it fly, singing the words from his song more slowly than usual, "I'll lift my bow and arrow in the air—there...Hit the bull's-eye..."

As Seeker leaned back on his bed, his backpack fell open, and he noticed his copy of the Great Book poking out of the top. Seeker reached for it and opened it to where the King had placed the bookmark. *Whoever saves his life, will lose it; and whoever loses his life will find it,* Seeker read aloud. "Hmm..."

The wicked dragon Itsalmine had crept unseen into Seeker's room. The situation had seemed pretty well under control—until now. "Not the Book!" Itsalmine was startled to see it. "Not *the* Book! Yikes! This calls for action!"

The dragon quickly slithered out from his hiding place and whispered, *Those words from the book have nothing to do with you, Seeker. It's just a book! And Doodle and Do's problem is not your problem. The King will look after them.*

"Doodle and Do's problem isn't my problem," Seeker said. "The King will look after them."

The dragon moved closer. *The King has lots of money. He wouldn't want you to give up your fifteen little coins.*

Seeker leaned back on his bed thoughtfully, "The King has lots of money. He wouldn't want me to give up my fifteen little coins."

Itsalmine whispered with convincing power, *You have worked so hard, and you deserve the best; it's only fair and right— that you have more, not less....*

Seeker sat straight up and looked around. "Those words! That voice! It's the dragon! Hey! Where are you, you ugly nose-picking dragon?" Seeker raced around his room, searching under his bed and in his closet.

Itsalmine struggled to escape Seeker's search, all the while trying to get his attention. *You deserve a bow and arrow set!*

Seeker clenched his teeth. "If I had a bow and arrow set right now, I know what I'd do with it! I would get you, you...But wait...I can't even see you! A bow and arrow wouldn't do any good."

Just then, a picture flashed through Seeker's mind. He saw the rich young man holding the blue leather pouch to his chest and turning away from the King. Then Seeker heard again the words the King spoke when he gave him his copy of the Great Book, "Reading my Book will help you to make good choices and wise decisions. It will help you to become a mighty warrior for me!"

Seeker laughed out loud and took hold of the Great Book. "I get it! I understand now! I can get rid of this dragon by making the right choice! I can be a mighty warrior right now—right here, right this very minute!"

Itsalmine was frantic. *Remember the CARNALville candy! Yummy, special secret recipe CARNALville candy! You can make a good choice, kid—you can choose to use your money to buy candy for all your friends! That would be a nice thing to do! Come on kid...*

Seeker shut his ears to the voice. Closing his eyes tightly and holding his Great Book close, Seeker took a deep breath and shouted boldly, "I choose to give up what I want to do, and I choose to do what is right!"

Itsalmine moaned as if he had been wounded. He shrank to the same size he had been when he first came to Seeker's life.

"I don't want to lose out like that rich guy!" Seeker shouted. "I will give up my money; I will give my fifteen coins to Doodle and Do!"

Itsalmine shrank even smaller as he roared in pain and slithered from the room. The miserable, nasty dragon cried and picked his nose all the way back to the CARNALville—all the way back to his master in the deep dark place beneath the trap door of Selfishness.

"Whew! That was intense!" Seeker sat down with a sigh of relief and smiled. "Doodle and Do, start packing your bags! You get to go and see your brother!"

He spilled the fifteen coins out onto his bed. "Now, let's see. If I just give the coins to Doodle and Do, they might not want to take them from me; or they might feel like they would have to pay me back...."

Seeker stood up and paced back and forth, trying to decide what to do. "Somehow," he said to himself, "it has to be a secret...it has to be a mystery. Yeah! And it has to be an adventure! I need to put the coins some place where Doodle and Do can find them...and in some kind of package that won't let them know who put them there!" He began searching in his closet for a container.

Then Seeker had an idea. He quickly opened his top dresser drawer where he kept the special little white box. He looked inside at the catalog picture of the bow and arrow set. "That's strange," Seeker said aloud. "I used to think the bow in this picture was really shiny gold...but now, it doesn't look very shiny or very gold! And you only get two arrows with it! I never noticed that!" He laughed. "I think while I'm saving up my money again, I'll shop around for a better deal!"

Seeker crumpled up the picture and tossed it into his trash can. Then he put the fifteen coins into the box and tied it up with a string. "Now," he said, reaching for a pen, "I'll write real big and slanted so they won't recognize my hand writing!"

Very carefully Seeker wrote, "To Doodle and Do from....?" across the top of the box.

As he drew the question mark, Seeker started feeling really, really, really excited. *Nobody knows! Nobody will ever know! he thought happily. Doodle and Do will be able to see their brother, and no one will ever, ever know where the money came from because it will be my secret.* He giggled and shook the box of jingling coins. *"My secret adventure."*

Chapter Seven

A few blocks from Seeker's home, not too far from the Big Rock at the base of the Straight and Narrow Path, Doodle and Do sat on their front porch. They had their hands propped under their chins thoughtfully. They were very serious. Not sad, not worried, just very serious. Tomorrow morning their parents would be going to see Daring, and still, no sign of the fifteen coins. Doodle had just checked the mailbox again.

"Why *do* you keep checking the mailbox?" Do asked.

Doodle shrugged his shoulders. "I don't know," he responded. "The King promised to look after us. He said that we could trust him and that no problem is too big—not even a problem called fifteen coins."

Do looked at Doodle, trying not to laugh. "But *do* you really think that's how the King will help us? *Do* you really think the fifteen coins will get here in the mailbox?"

Doodle shrugged. "It doesn't matter how the King gets them here. What matters is that we trust him! And even though it's hard to trust..."

Then both boys smiled, and their serious mood left them as they said together, "It's what we're going to *do!*" Laughing, they went into their house.

Meanwhile, Seeker ran down the stairs, out from his house, and through the village streets toward Doodle and Do's home.

A tall hedge bordered their yard. *Perfect!* Seeker thought as he crept along beside the hedge. When he reached the gate of Doodle and Do's yard he peeked out, carefully making sure that no one was there to see him. Excitement seemed ready to burst inside Seeker as he tiptoed up to the mailbox and then very carefully and very quietly set the little white box inside.

Seeker could hardly keep from laughing as he pictured Doodle and Do discovering the little package in their mailbox. He struggled to keep quiet as he crept back around the corner of the hedge and...bumped into...

...the King.

"Oh!" Seeker cried in surprise, then quickly composed himself. "Oh, hello there, King! So, uh, what are you doing here in the village today?"

The King smiled one of his mysterious smiles. "I had to come down and say *thank you* to someone."

"Oh. Who did you have to say thank you to?" asked Seeker. "What for?"

The King looked around to make sure no one was listening. Then he whispered, "I had to come and say thank you for fifteen coins in a little white box tied up with a string." The King smiled, leaned forward, and winked at Seeker.

Seeker could hardly believe his ears. "King! That's my secret adventure! You won't tell anyone, will you, King? Will you? How did you know, anyway?"

The King led Seeker over to the Big Rock at the base of the Straight and Narrow Path. "Seeker, you will find out, as you read your copy of the Great Book, that whenever you give something away that *really* matters to you—you've actually given it to me."

"I have?" Seeker said.

The King nodded as he sat down on the Big Rock.

"Listen closely, Seeker," the King said. "There is a battle every day—whether to seek to keep your life or give it to me. The inner battle of your heart is the hardest battle you will ever fight, Seeker, and no one sees that war except for me. And *I* say that you are a mighty warrior!"

"I am?" Seeker asked in surprise.

Then the King did something that *really* surprised Seeker. He stood behind him, turned him toward the village, and put his big hands over Seeker's hands. Then together, they lifted up an imaginary bow, set an imaginary arrow in it, pulled back the string, and aimed.

Suddenly, with the King's help, Seeker was able to see Doodle and Do's front porch. He could see Doodle coming out from their house and going to check the mailbox...just one more time. Seeker watched Doodle open the door of the mailbox, and he watched the boy's surprise when he saw the package. Seeker could hear Doodle call to his brother, Do, to come and look at the strange little white box.

Seeker felt the King's arms, strong around his; and he felt the King pull back the invisible arrow...just a bit farther. "Ready, Seeker?" the King whispered. Seeker nodded, his eyes filling with happy tears.

They pulled back the arrow just a little bit more, and then, with a surge of strength and power like Seeker had never felt before, they let go. "Hit the bull's-eye!" the King whispered with laughter in his voice.

The invisible arrow hit the little white box exactly the same moment that Doodle and Do untied the string and fifteen coins fell out into their hands.

The King wrapped his great arms around Seeker, and together they watched the two happy boys talking excitedly about how the King had solved their big problem in one little answer—a little white box tied up with a string! They listened as Doodle and Do wondered how the little box actually got into their mailbox; they talked about getting to see their brother.

"We get to see Daring! We really *do!*"

"Time to start packing for the trip, Doodle!"

"It's what we're going to *do!*"

Then Doodle and Do turned and ran up the walk and into their house to tell their parents the good news.

Seeker looked up at the King, and his eyes were shining. "We hit the bull's-eye, King!" The King nodded.

Then Seeker took both of the King's hands and touched the old faded scars. "That's what you did, isn't it, King?" Seeker said quietly, "You *really* hit the bull's-eye! You didn't keep your life. You gave it up, and you really found it!"

The King smiled yet another one of his mysterious smiles. Then he and Seeker turned and walked together through the streets of Peace and Harmony in his Kingdom.

You might be wondering what happened to Doodle and Do and their brother, Daring, and whether or not Seeker ever got a bow and arrow set...well, that's another adventure in the Kingdom.

Think About the Story

The King's Great Book is another name for the Bible. The words in the Bible will help you get to know King Jesus; and your life will really be a never-ending adventure!

Talk to the King

"King Jesus, sometimes my toys, my clothes, my money, and all my stuff seem so important to me. Help me to see what really matters. Help me be willing to give and to share cheerfully whenever I get the chance! And I know that each time I give to someone, I'm really giving it to you!"

Read from the King's Great Book—Matthew 16:25

If you seek to keep your life, you'll lose it, lose it; But give your life to Jesus and life you'll find! Matthew 16, (clap) verse 25! (Great Book Paraphrase)

- **Matthew 6:3-4: Now that's an adventure!**

- **Matthew 6:19-21: Treasures forever**

- **Matthew 19:16-22: The story of the Rich Young Ruler**

Part Four

In Search of Wanderer

Chapter One

S eeker looked again at the photograph of his family. Why couldn't things have stayed the way they were in that picture? Why did his dad have to go away?

Seeker's father's name was Wanderer. At one time, Wanderer lived in the Kingdom. He used to live at home...but not anymore. Seeker wasn't sure what had happened; he just knew that he *really* missed his dad. With a deep sigh, Seeker tucked the picture back into his shirt pocket and kept walking toward Royal Harbor.

Just then, two familiar voices called, "Hey Seeker! Wait for us!" Seeker turned to see his friends, Doodle and Do, running toward him. Seeker waved and smiled as the two brothers tried to out-*do* each other at running. Doodle reached him first, excitedly holding up two lanterns. "Look what I have, Seeker!"

Do came panting up from behind, also holding two lanterns. "Me, too! Look at my lanterns! Daring told us to bring these in case we need extra ones for the club meeting today!"

Seeker was impressed. "Lanterns? I wonder where Daring is planning to take us this time?"

Doodle and Do's brother, Daring, was a royal officer in the King's service on the sea. Daring used to be gone for months at a time, but now he lived in Royal Harbor and only went sailing when the King sent him out on special adventures.

"*Do* you remember the time when we *really* needed fifteen coins so we could go see Daring?" Doddle asked.

"I sure *do!*" his brother responded.

"I'll *never* forget that!" Seeker said. "But now you can see your brother whenever you want! We all can! Let's get going, or we'll be late!" Seeker said.

The boys hurried toward Royal Harbor for the Adventure Club meeting. Once a week after school, Seeker and his friends had been getting together aboard the tall sailing ship, *The Adventurer*. Daring had served so faithfully that the King had given him his very own ship. Now in port at Royal Harbor, *The Adventurer* had become a favorite meeting place for the children.

When they reached Royal Harbor, Seeker slowed to a walk, but Doodle and Do raced toward the pier where their other friends were leaning against the railing. Giggles, Gladness, and Glee were laughing, like usual. Dawdle and Slow were quietly tossing cracker crumbs to the sea gulls. HopeSo, KnowSo, and Yes were trying to guess how big the ship was and how fast it could go.

Seeker breathed in deeply the saltwater air and smiled as he watched Doodle and Do showing their lanterns to the other children. Then Seeker looked past his friends to the familiar wooden ship tied to the dock. Gentle waves slapped the sides of *The Adventurer* and its three huge sails billowed in the wind, as if longing to leave the port. Daring was standing on the deck waving. "Come aboard!" he shouted.

Everyone laughed and waved back as they hurried over the gangplank and onto the deck of the tall ship. "Wait for me!" The children turned to see Moira hurrying across the pier. (Seeker's sister, Moira, had been helping Daring every week with the Adventure Club.)

"OK," Daring nodded. "Everyone is here! Do you remember the song we learned last week?"

"I should *hope* so!" said HopeSo.

"I *know* so!" said KnowSo, in his most confident voice.

Their sister laughed, "*Yes, yes* of course we do! It's called 'The Attitude of Gratitude'!"

"And it's what we're going to *do!*" called Doodle and Do as they led the others in singing:

> *I have an attitude of gratitude!*
> *I have an attitude of gratitude!*
> *I have an attitude of gratitude—*
> *in my heart all the time.*
> *Doodle do do do, Doodle do do do*
> *Doodle do do do,*
> *Doodle do do do!*

Doodle and Do did a little sailor jig during the last chorus. The other children laughed until their stomach hurt; and the more they laughed, the more Doodle and Do added to their dance! The two brothers loved having an audience.

"Wonderful!" Moira said, applauding, "And now for the Adventure Club drill! Attention!" The children lined up and saluted.

"Adventure Club members have an attitude of gratitude!" she called.

"Attitude of gratitude!" the children responded together.

"Adventure Club members overcome obstacles with opposites!" she announced.

The children nodded and saluted. "Overcome obstacles with opposites!"

"You overcome darkness with...?" Moira asked.

"Light!" the children shouted together.

"You overcome evil with...?"

"Good!"

"You overcome greed with...?"

"Giving!"

"You overcome sadness with...?"

"Gladness!"

As everyone laughed and patted Gladness on the back, Daring called, "It's time for today's adventure! Each of you will need to carry a lantern with you. Help yourselves to the ones sitting over there on the wooden crates, and Doodle and Do brought extra ones so we would have enough."

As the children each picked up a lantern they talked excitedly. "Where are we going today?" "It must be some place dark if we need lanterns."

Yes was nervous. "I hope it's not too dark—I get scared sometimes when it's dark!"

Moira put an arm around the younger girl's shoulder and smiled reassuringly. "Don't worry—we're all together!"

Daring picked up the picnic basket. "After the adventure we'll come back here and give you time to work on your model ships!"

Seeker was relieved. "Great! I've almost finished mine, and I want to take it home today!" The children had all been working hard the past few weeks on building small wooden ships.

They followed Daring and Moira over the gangplank and back onto the shore. "Wh-wh-where are we going?" asked Dawdle.

Daring smiled at Dawdle. "Caves," he responded, in a low mysterious voice.

"Caves?" the children echoed.

Daring nodded. "Caves."

Chapter Two

Between Royal Harbor and the Castle of Joy and Peace was an underground passageway with a maze of tunnels and caves. Daring had spent many childhood days exploring these. Today he led Moira and the children to a steep cliff at the edge of Royal Harbor where an entrance to the passageway was hidden behind some trees and bushes. When they reached the entrance, the children were very happy to find someone waiting to meet them....

"King! Hi!" Giggles, Gladness, and Glee reached him first and laughed as the King picked each of them up and twirled them in the air. The others all crowded around for a group hug.

Then the King opened the door to the passageway and smiled one of his mysterious smiles. "Shall we?" he asked, and everyone followed the King through the entrance.

"S-Sure is d-d-dark in here!" called Slow as she and the others lit their lanterns.

Glee laughed and held her lantern high. "You overcome darkness with...?"

"Light!" the others responded.

Yes reached out to the King. "And you overcome fear of the dark by holding the King's hand!"

The King smiled. "Alright now everyone, there are hundreds of tunnels that lead off from the main passageway, so follow me and stay close together!" The King led the way through the rocky hall. Daring, Moira, and the children "oohed" and "ahhed" over the beautiful rock formations. Stalactites and stalagmites decorated the tunnel with a gold glow under the light of the lanterns.

After many long moments of walking, the King stooped to enter a low doorway. "Cave," KnowSo whispered knowingly. Yes nodded. She had been walking confidently far down the line, but now hurried once again to take hold of the King's hand.

The children were surprised and happy to find a low rocky shelf around the wall of the cave. It was a perfect place to sit down.

The King stood in the middle of the cave, and everyone looked at him. "I want you to experience something for a few moments," he said. "Darkness."

"Darkness?" Yes echoed, holding more tightly to his hand.

"Darkness," the King repeated. He looked around at the children's faces and asked, "Do you trust me?"

"Yes, we *do!*" everyone responded, with Doodle and Do's voices loudest of all.

"Then blow out your lanterns," said the King.

Everyone blew out their lanterns. Immediately, they were in total darkness. It was darker than any darkness they had ever been in before. Giggles, Gladness, and Glee giggled nervously.

"This is how some people live their lives," the King said, "In complete darkness."

"That would be very scary," Yes's voice trembled slightly.

"You know my Kingdom as Joy and Peace," said the King. It is also the Kingdom of Light. Everyone who really knows me lives in the Light. But the people who don't know me..."

"Live in Darkness." KnowSo said, finishing the sentence.

"That would be a very sad place to live," Moira said softly. "I never want to live in Darkness!"

"Stay close to me, Moira," said the King, "and you *won't* live in Darkness."

"Did the people of Greed live in the Darkness, King?" KnowSo asked, remembering how the children had destroyed the dragon Greed with giving and the people moved to Generosity.

"Yes," the King responded. "And many years ago, your families lived in the Darkness of Fear."

"My mom told me all about that," said Seeker. "The dragon Fear controlled everyone there!"

"Please don't talk anymore about dragons!" Yes said, clutching tightly to the King's hand.

"*Do* you think there are more dragons out there, King?" Doodle asked excitedly.

"Many more dragons, Doodle," the King answered. "They rule the Darkness and try to keep people blinded, so they cannot see my Light."

With that the King lit a lantern. The warm glow shone on his face as he spoke solemnly, "Too many people spend their lives in the Darkness, going through a maze of endless tunnels and caverns." Then the King looked directly at Moira and Seeker. "Some people spend their lives *wandering*, never finding their way to Joy and Peace in my Kingdom."

When the King said the word *wandering*, Seeker and Moira caught their breath. "Wandering," Seeker whispered. Moira reached out and gave her brother's hand a quick squeeze. Seeker touched the pocket where the picture of his family was safely tucked. "Wanderer," he said, looking at Moira.

Moira felt the familiar stab of pain in her heart. Although she had tried to be strong for Seeker's sake, the long months without her father had been difficult for Moira. Lately, she had been telling herself to just accept the fact that he was gone and get on with her life. She had been trying to overcome the pain by not thinking about it; but it wasn't working very well.

Daring and the children explored the cave, and the King sat down beside Seeker and Moira. "Dad is living in Darkness, isn't he, King?" Seeker asked.

The King nodded and Moira said, "Dragons. Are there dragons keeping him in the Darkness, King?"

The King nodded again. "There are dragons, Moira," he said, "but they aren't making your father stay in the Darkness. He is choosing to stay there." The King looked deep into Moira's eyes and said, "Living in Darkness or living in my Kingdom is a choice that each person must make."

"My heart hurts, King," Seeker said. "It *really* hurts."

The King very gently touched Seeker's heart. A deep warmth filled him, and Seeker felt his pain get smaller. "Thanks, King," he whispered.

Then the King reached out to touch Moira's heart, but she stopped him, took hold of both his hands, and said, "It's OK, King. I'm fine."

A look of concern flashed through the King's eyes. "You must come and talk to me about how you *really* feel, Moira," he said.

Moira nodded and quickly wiped away the tears that had suddenly spilled out of her eyes. "OK, King, I'll do that...sometime soon.... I promise. I'll come and talk to you..."

By now, some of the other children had been watching quietly. "*Do* you think Wanderer will ever come home?" Do whispered.

"I *hope* so!" said HopeSo.

"I *know* so!" said KnowSo confidently.

"Yes, yes of course he will!" Yes nodded, going to sit close to Moira. Glee followed her and the two young girls looked sadly at Moira. They loved Seeker's sister and wished they could help.

After exploring a few more tunnels and caves, the King led them out through the passageways, and back toward Royal Harbor. When they reached the entrance, the King waved goodbye and the children continued on to *The Adventurer*. They were anxious to get to work on their model ships.

Chapter Three

Seeker hummed the "Attitude of Gratitude" song as he tightened the sails, attached the anchor, and set a miniature wooden steering wheel in place on his boat. Then he took his paintbrush and carefully put the finishing touches on the wooden hull.

Finally, with a happy sigh, Seeker proudly carried the little model ship over to his sister. Moira was impressed. "Seeker! It's wonderful! It looks just like the real *Adventurer!*"

"Do you think so, Moira?" he asked, pleased. "I *really* worked hard on it! I'm done now. Can I leave?"

"Sure," Moira said, "I'll see you at home!"

As Seeker walked down the path toward the Village of Peace and Harmony, he thought about the "Attitude of Gratitude" song. He had sung the words so many times, but had never really thought about what they meant, until now.

"Hmm..." Seeker said aloud, "An attitude of gratitude in my heart all the time. I wonder how you can have an attitude of gratitude in your heart *all* the time? How are you supposed to be thankful *all* the time?

Especially...especially..."

Seeker sat down on a rock near the path and set his model ship beside him. He reached inside his shirt pocket and pulled out the little picture of his family. On one side of the photograph were Moira and his mother, Contentment; on the other side were Seeker and his father...Wanderer.

Seeker shook his head and held back tears that began to form in his eyes. *How are you supposed to have an attitude of gratitude about something like this? How are you supposed to be*

131

happy when you haven't seen your dad for a long, long time? He
never writes; he doesn't even send you a birthday card! How are
you supposed to be glad that your dad's name is Wanderer!

Seeker angrily stuffed the picture back into his shirt pocket.
"I don't feel like going home yet," he said aloud. "I think I'll go
and see if my boat will float."

He picked up the model ship and went to one of his favorite
places, the stream behind the castle.

Seeker had a special spot at the stream where he and the
King often went fishing and skipping rocks. The first day when
Seeker had begun to really get to know him, the King had
brought him here. The King had explained how water from the
Throne Room fountain tumbled down an underground waterfall
and flowed out into the stream, where everyone in the Kingdom
could enjoy the clear fresh water.

Seeker pulled his shoes off and rolled up his pant legs and
then, very carefully, set the small wooden boat onto the water.
Sure enough—it floated! Up and down it bobbed along, like a
real ship out on the open sea. Seeker sat down on the grassy
shore beside the stream and watched. "Hmm...I sure wish Dad
could see my boat! He always liked making things, too. We sure
had some good times together."

Seeker lay down on the grass and rolled over onto his back.
White puffy clouds moved slowly across the sky above him.
Seeker liked to watch clouds and think about what each fluffy
shape reminded him of. Today many of the clouds were in the
shapes of animals. Seeker thought about the wooden carvings
on his bedroom shelf that his dad had made for him. There were
dozens of little animals and all sizes of castles and miniature
wooden soldiers; but Seeker's favorite carving was one of himself
and his dad running together across a hill. Seeker's eyes filled
with tears and he shut them tightly. "Dad," he whispered. "Dad,

I miss you so much! Will you ever come home? Will I ever get to see you again?"

Seeker opened his eyes and blinked away the tears so that he could see. The clouds still moved slowly overhead. He looked at one especially big fluffy cloud. It looked like a ship...

A ship!

Oh, no! Seeker had been thinking so much about his father that he had forgotten to watch his model ship! He jumped to his feet and ran along the shore, desperately looking at the water. A short way downstream he saw the little boat. There it was— smashed against some rocks. Seeker hurried into the water and picked up the broken pieces.

"My boat! My boat! I worked so hard; and now it's wrecked!" The tears he had been holding back wouldn't stay inside any longer. "My boat! My boat!" he cried.

Then Seeker heard someone whistling. Oh, no! He didn't want anyone to know he had been crying, and he didn't want to have to explain why. Using his shirt sleeve to wipe his nose, Seeker blinked hard and got ready to face whoever was coming. The whistling grew louder. Seeker took a deep breath and looked down the shore.

It was the King.

There he stood on the banks of the stream, looking at Seeker. The King smiled. It was a very, very gentle smile, and he kept whistling. The song he was whistling was "Attitude of Gratitude." All of a sudden Seeker felt angry. He ran toward the King, threw the broken boat on the ground and cried, "Don't you sing that song! It's an awful song! An awful song!"

The King reached out his great arms toward Seeker, but Seeker was filled with such hurt and anger that he pushed the King's arms away and pounded on the King's chest with his fists. The King stood very quietly and just let him do that. Then the tears came again, this time in such a flood that Seeker didn't even try to hold them back.

With a deep sob, Seeker's fists fell to his sides, and the King very gently took the boy in his arms, held him close, and just let him cry. The King put his hand on Seeker's heart. He had touched Seeker's heart earlier when they were in the cave, but now he seemed to touch pain that was even deeper inside. The King didn't ask Seeker to stop crying; he just held him and waited until Seeker had cried enough tears to wash some of the sadness and anger away.

Finally, Seeker blew his nose on a tissue that the King handed to him and said, "King, I don't understand. How am I supposed to have an attitude of gratitude? How am I supposed to be thankful? Look at my boat!" Seeker picked the pieces up from the ground. "I worked so hard; and now look at it—it's broken! How am I supposed to be thankful about that?"

"You can be thankful, Seeker, because I know how to fix boats."

Seeker was surprised. "You do?"

The King nodded. "Yes. In fact, if you give me all the pieces and *really* trust me, I can fix *anything* that's broken."

"You can?" Seeker whispered, "OK, King."

Seeker lifted up all the broken pieces of his boat, and the King put them carefully into the pocket of his cloak, and they walked together toward the village. The "Attitude of Gratitude" song began to stir in Seeker's heart, slowly at first, but then stronger and stronger. He whistled with the King all the way to Peace and Harmony.

Chapter Four

When they reached Seeker's house, Moira came out and said, "Seeker, don't go in there. Mom's crying again." She turned to the King, "King, would you talk to our mom? Sometimes she misses Dad so much...and we don't know what to say to her."

The King gave Moira a hug. "Yes, I'll talk to her. That's one reason I walked Seeker home today!" The King knocked softly on the door and then went into the house.

Seeker and Moira sat down together on the back step. "Moira, do you think we'll ever see Dad again?" Seeker asked.

"I don't know Seeker," Moira replied. "He sure has been gone for a long time. I wish he'd write a letter or something. I *really* miss him."

"Yeah, me too." Seeker sighed.

Moira looked at her brother for a moment and then spoke carefully. "Seeker...I think it's time for you to accept the facts. We might never see Dad again. Seeker, you need to realize that our family is broken."

Seeker sat straight up and looked at his sister with amazement. "What did you say?"

"I said our family's broken, Seeker." Moira repeated sadly.

"Hooray!" Seeker cheered and jumped to his feet.

Moira stood beside him, confused. "Hooray? What do you mean 'hooray'?"

"I was just talking to the King! He said he could fix *anything* that's broken! It's a long story, but the King came and found me at the stream—my boat was broken..."

"Your boat was broken?" Moira repeated, shocked. "You mean your model ship? What happened?"

"Never mind right now!" Seeker said quickly, "The important thing is that the King said that he could fix *anything* that's broken! That means he could fix our family!"

Moira shook her head. "Oh, now, just a minute," she said, "I know that the King is *really* powerful—but fix our family? I don't know, Seeker. That's pretty hard, even for the King."

"No, it's not too hard! If he can fix anything that's broken, then he can fix our family! I know it! Listen, Moira, we've never *really* asked him! It's like we've just given up on Dad; we haven't *really* talked to the King about him!"

Moira was thoughtful. "You're right," she said. "We've never *really* asked..."

"I have an idea!" Seeker said. "We could go to the Secret Place—you and I together—to the Secret Place every day and *really* ask the King to bring Dad home!"

Moira smiled her agreement. "OK, Seeker! It's certainly worth a try!"

The Secret Place is a special place where people can go and talk to the King. They don't always see him, but he is *always* there. Seeker had his very own Secret Place in one of the castle towers, and he and Moira began meeting there every day. They went the first day, but they didn't see the King. Second day—no King. Third day, fourth day, fifth day, sixth day...still no King. Finally, on the seventh day, they decided to go to the Secret Place instead of eating lunch. When they arrived, the door was open and the King was waiting for them...

"I had to make sure you *really* wanted this," he said, "because it is *not* going to be easy."

The King led Seeker and Moira to the Window of the Secret Place and opened the golden shutters. (The Window of the Secret Place is where the King shows his people the way things *really* are, not the way they appear to be.) To Seeker and Moira's surprise, although it was lunch-time, through the Window they saw a beautiful night sky. Thousands of twinkling stars shone in the darkness. The King pointed, "Do you see those stars? I made them! And I call each one by name!"

Seeker and Moira looked up at the King with awe. "Wow!" they said together.

Then they looked again through the Window of the Secret Place, and instead of the night sky, now they saw a stormy ocean. Lightning and thunder filled the scene, and powerful waves came crashing against the Window. Moira and Seeker hid behind the King so they wouldn't get wet.

The King lifted his hand and spoke to the storm, "Peace—be still," he said. And the winds and the waves went calm.

Seeker and Moira again looked up at the King with awe, "Wow!"

The next scene they saw through the Window was a dark village. It seemed very sad and empty, and a lonely wind echoed through the streets. Seeker and Moira shivered. As they continued to peer through the dim light, they saw an old building that looked like a store. The sign above the front door was faded, and all the windows were boarded shut.

They looked more closely and were unable to see inside the store. It was filled with piles of lumber and tools and stacks of books and papers. Everything was covered in a blanket of dust and cobwebs. On a table in the middle of the room, the low flicker of a lantern was struggling to fight off the darkness.

And then, Seeker and Moira saw something else.

There, sitting on a chair, with chains around his body and his eyes half closed, was a man. His beard and hair had not been trimmed for a very long time, and at first Moira and Seeker didn't recognize him. Then Seeker gasped, "Dad! That's Dad!"

"Dad?" Moira echoed, "No, that can't be Dad; he doesn't have a beard...Wait a minute, Seeker, you're right. That *is* Dad! But he looks so awful!"

They watched Wanderer for a moment, shocked at his appearance. Then Seeker pointed and cried, "Look! Dragons!"

Two incredibly ugly dragons snarled as they came to stand by Wanderer. The dragons laughed viciously as they pulled the chains tighter, but Wanderer didn't seem to notice. He was almost asleep...

Seeker understood something about fighting dragons. When he saw those awful creatures beside his father, courage filled his heart! He would come against the dragons in the name of the King! Seeker began to roll up his sleeves when he felt a gentle hand on his shoulder. "No, Seeker," said the King. "Not this time. Your father *likes* those dragons."

"He *likes* those dragons?!" echoed Seeker and Moira together. "What! How can he *like* them?"

Your father is living in a place called Despair. He never learned to overcome the obstacles; now the obstacles have overcome *him*...and he *likes* it that way. To him, it feels like he is in a safe place. He *likes* living in the Darkness."

"He could get away if he wanted to," said Moira as she looked closer. "The chains aren't that tight. I guess maybe the dragons just make Dad *feel* like he can't move."

"How can they do that?" asked Seeker. "Why are those dragons so powerful, King? What are their names, anyway?"

"The dragons are Discouragement and Bitterness," the King explained. "When they first came to your father, they were quite small; but the more he listened to their voices, the stronger they became."

Seeker remembered the last dragon he had fought—the dragon Itsalmine. Seeker had saved up coins to buy something that he *really* wanted—a bow and arrow set. The dragon had tried to convince Seeker that the money was all his and that he deserved the best bow and arrow in the village, even though Doodle and Do desperately needed the same exact amount of money. Seeker shuddered, remembering. "King, if I would have kept listening to Itsalmine, would he have grown stronger?"

The King nodded. Seeker gulped and said, "What a scary thought. And by now I would have been...I would have been..."

"On your way to a very sad and very dark place, Seeker," said the King.

"Like Dad?" Moira asked.

"A similar place," the King nodded. "Your father lives in Despair...and he wants to stay that way. He has given up. Discouragement and Bitterness have overwhelmed him."

Moira looked up with tearful eyes. "But King! Can't you *make* him leave that place?"

The King shook his head sadly, "No. Not until he *really* wants me to." Then the King wrapped his great arms around Seeker and Moira and began to sing...

> *Behold I hold the universe within my hands;*
> *The mighty ocean waves are mine,*
> *I command them!*
> *But when it comes to wandering hearts...*
> *Those I will not claim*
> *Until they really want me to...*
> *I just stand...and wait.*
> *Oh how I long for them to come to me;*
> *Oh how I long for them to run to me!*
> *Oh how I long for them to really see my Light—*
> *but they are blinded...*
> *Oh how I long for them to come to me;*
> *Oh how I long for them to run to me!*
> *Oh how I long for them to really see my Light.*

As the King finished his song, Moira turned to him in desperation. "King, that's our father! We can't just leave him there! There must be something we can do! Isn't there something we can do, King?"

The King looked at Seeker and Moira's earnest young faces, and nodded. "Yes. There is something you can do. I want you to continue to meet here every day in the Secret Place; and as you do, those dragons will not be able to lie to your father anymore. And I want you to really believe that your father will read the Great Book. He used to read it. If he would just open it, I would speak to him."

"All right, King! We'll do it!"

Chapter Five

S eeker and Moira continued to meet faithfully in the Secret Place, talking to the King about their father. The days and weeks passed. Then one morning, the King told the children that it was a special day—he and Daring and Moira were going to take them on a real adventure out on the open sea!

Everyone packed a lunch and waved good-bye to their friends and families on the shore. The boat left the dock and went out, out, out onto the water. They sailed for a long time, and Seeker and his friends took turns steering the ship. They stood on the deck, letting the wind blow through their hair and watching the waves slap the sides of the great ship with gentle rhythm. Doodle and Do led everyone in singing the "Attitude of Gratitude" song, trying to do their sailor jig while the ship rocked back and forth.

Around noon, after everyone had finished lunch, the King came up from the captain's quarters in the lower part of the ship. "We are on the Sea of Sadness," he said, pulling a knapsack onto his back. "I must leave you for a while. If a storm should come up while I'm gone, I want you to overcome it with...?"

"Gladness!" the children responded quickly. But they didn't slap Gladness on the back like usual; they were too curious.

"Where are you going, King?" KnowSo wanted to know.

"What are you going to *do?*" Doodle asked.

The King didn't answer, he just smiled and winked. Then he climbed down the rope ladder on the side of the ship's hull, and into a little rowboat that was tied alongside. Moira,

Daring, and the children watched the King row the boat until a fog rolled in across the Sea of Sadness, and the King disappeared from their sight.

Chapter Six

Through the dense fog, the King rowed to an island. He pulled the boat up onto the shore and tied it securely. Then, glancing around to make sure that no one was watching, the King reached inside the knapsack and pulled out an ordinary-looking peasant cloak. He removed his royal cloak, folded it, and placed it inside the knapsack in the rowboat.

Then the King put the peasant cloak over his royal clothing and turned toward a path leading through the forest. A rugged sign pointed the way to the Village Despair.

The King smiled one of his most mysterious smiles. He pulled the hood of the peasant cloak up over his head and stepped onto the shaded path...toward Despair.

Despair is a terrible place where too many people live. It is sad, dark, and very lonely. But in that place, the King heard someone whistling the "Attitude of Gratitude" song! He walked through the streets until he reached the place where the whistling was coming from.

There, right in the middle of Despair, was a freshly painted store. The windows were clean and shiny. A brand new sign was hanging above the door: "Wanderer's Woodworking."

The King buttoned his cloak and made sure that his hood was in place. Then, after pausing for a moment with another of his mysterious smiles, the King walked through the door...

The store looked much different than when Seeker and Moira had seen it through the Window of the Secret Place. Everything was clean and tidy. The dust and cobwebs were gone; the tools were neatly in their places; the books and papers were organized; and the Great Book was open on the table near the bright glow of the lantern.

In a far corner, the dragons, Discouragement and Bitterness, were gagged and chained! The very chains they had used on Wanderer now covered them! When the dragons saw the King, they squirmed in pain and cried, "Mmpphh!" The King smiled again.

Wanderer was bent over his workbench, busily making some bows and arrows. He looked up, saw the stranger in a cloak, and reached out his hand in greeting, "Good day, sir! My name is Wanderer. And you are...?"

"I am...*Answer!*" the King said, shaking Wanderer's hand firmly.

"Well, it's good to meet you, Answer! Is there anything I can help you with?"

The King picked up an arrow. "Tell me about what you have been working on today."

Wanderer proudly held up a bow and another arrow. "I make the best bows and arrows in the land, sir. Some of them are heavy and strong; others are lightweight, and all have great accuracy and balance. Each one is made for a special reason—a special purpose!"

"*Really?*" the King spoke thoughtfully, as he inspected the arrow. "You know, that reminds me of people. Every person is made for a special reason—a special purpose." The King set the arrow down and turned toward Wanderer.

"What is *your* special purpose?"

Wanderer was surprised and suddenly felt very embarrassed. "Special purpose? Why...I don't know, sir! I suppose I have searched all my life for my special purpose; but I've never found it."

The King walked over to the Great Book, open on the table.

The lantern beside it glowed even more brightly as the King approached. "Have you searched here, Wanderer?"

"I used to, sir," replied Wanderer, "and I have been again lately." Wanderer walked across the room and stood beside Answer and the Great Book. "You know, it tells the most amazing story about a King!"

"*Really?* Tell me about this King."

"Well, it seems that the King loved his people so much that he left his throne, left his Kingdom, and went right down to where they were!"

"Hmm..." said the King softly, "then what happened?"

"He made himself look like one of the people," Wanderer said, "He wore a disguise—so they didn't realize who he was..."

"I see," said the King.

Wanderer picked up the Great Book and continued, "The King did miracles and told stories about his Kingdom. He explained to the people how much the King loved them—but they didn't understand..."

Wanderer shook his head sadly. "They didn't understand. I was just reading today how the people turned against him. They took nails and put them into his hands and his feet and they...they killed him!" Wanderer set the Book back on the table, shaking his head in dismay. "They *killed* Him."

Slowly, the King pushed back the hood of his cloak and spoke softly, "He didn't stay dead, Wanderer."

Wanderer gasped, "Wh...what...?"

Then the King held out his hands, revealing two old and faded scars. And Wanderer whispered in amazement, "King! You are the King...and not just the King; you are the *real* King... You are the King in the Great Book!"

The King nodded and spoke with gentle strength. "The King did not stay dead, Wanderer...and he is still the *Answer* to *everything* you have *ever* searched for."

Wanderer looked into the eyes of the King, took hold of his wounded hands, and knelt down. "Your Majesty," he said.

And as he knelt, the dragons in the corner grew smaller and smaller and smaller...until they disappeared.

Chapter Seven

Meanwhile, back on the ship, Moira, Daring, and the children were struggling to keep afloat. A raging storm had hit the Sea of Sadness. Winds of Weariness were blowing and waves were crashing against the ship with such force that it was difficult to keep standing.

Everyone was trying hard to overcome the sadness with gladness; they were walking around, holding onto the railing with big grins on their faces, but the storm just seemed too powerful.

"We have to do something to calm the storm!" Moira shouted to Daring. "We must fight it together—we need a song!"

"A song?!" Daring echoed. "A song! Yes—I have the perfect song!"

Daring shouted over the howling wind to the children, "Listen everyone, and join in singing!"

> *I will overcome the Sea of Sadness;*
> *Before it overcomes me*
> *When the Winds of Weariness blow*
> *And the waves rise up, I will sing,*
> *I will sing, I will sing!*

Gladness held on tightly to the railing and struggled across the deck toward Moira and Daring. "I know this song!" he shouted. "This song is how my parents got my name! This song is how I became Gladness!"

Daring smiled and reached out to take the boy's hand. Daring knew how hard life had been for Gladness...how he had been very sick when he was a baby, and now he walked with a limp. The beginning of his life had been very stormy, but in the middle of it all, his parents had named him Gladness.

Daring squeezed the boy's hand more tightly and shouted through the driving rain and wind. "Sing it, Gladness! Sing to the sadness!"

Gladness lifted his voice, singing louder than the wind.

> *The King has given me a heart of gladness*
> *To face every storm that life may bring*
> *I will dance and lift my hands;*
> *I will laugh and I'll sing!*
> *I will laugh and I'll sing...*
> *I will laugh and I'll sing!*

As he sang, Gladness began to laugh. He laughed and he laughed and he laughed. He laughed so hard that everyone else just had to join in! Soon they were having so much fun laughing and singing that it didn't matter how strong the storm was; it didn't matter how great the sadness was!

Then Seeker made a discovery—he found that he could actually sing to the waves! He leaned over the side of the ship, chose a wave and called straight toward it, "Sing!" and the wave went down!

"Hey everyone!" he shouted. "You can sing to the waves! You can sing directly to the storm and your song is stronger than it is! Look!"

Seeker leaned over the railing of the ship, aimed, and shouted, "Sing!" The wave went calm. The others were impressed. Soon everyone was using their song to overcome the storm.

Seeker and Moira were standing together on the side of the ship, singing to the last few waves..."Sing!"..."Sing!" when Seeker looked off into the distance and suddenly cried, "Look! The King is coming back! The King is coming back!" Seeker looked more closely and caught his breath. "And...and...he's not...alone...!"

Seeker and Moira stood together with their hands clenched tightly and watched as the little rowboat got closer and closer. Daring and the children crowded around them, trying to see. "Who's with the King?" everyone wondered. The closer the rowboat came, the more tightly Seeker and Moira clenched each other's hands. The person with the King was their father.

Everyone watched in silence as the rowboat came alongside *The Adventurer*. They watched as the King tied the boat securely to the ship and he and Wanderer climbed up the rope ladder. Then everyone stood back as Wanderer walked over to his children and stood silently in front of them. A moment of awkward silence passed, and then their father began to cry.

"Moira...Seeker. I'm so sorry," he said, "I am so sorry. I never learned to overcome the obstacles in my life. Instead, I let the obstacles overcome me. I turned away from the King, and I got lost in the Darkness. It was like wandering through a maze of endless tunnels and caverns...and I let Discouragement and Bitterness rule my life. Please, will you forgive me?"

Moira and Seeker nodded through their tears and rushed to put their arms around him. "We forgive you, Dad! We forgive you."

Their father hugged Moira and Seeker close and said, "The King has come to me, and he's given me a new heart, and a new name! From now on, I am Steadfast!"

As Moira and Seeker stood in their father's arms, Daring and the children happily gathered around and joined in for a group hug. Then Steadfast reached into a satchel and pulled out a polished wooden bow and five arrows with blue and red feathers on the ends. He turned to Seeker and said, "I wanted to give these to you, son. I've been working on this special set, and I was thinking about you the whole time while I worked. The King told me that you would *really* like them."

"The King was right! Yes Dad, I *really* like them! Thanks! Wow...these are nicer than any I've ever seen..."

Moira's eyes were shining. "Dad, it will be so good to have you back at home!"

"Well, Moira, the King and I talked about where I should live now. I'm back in the Kingdom, but I won't go home...not just yet..." Steadfast looked over at the King, who winked at him. "The King has given me a new name, but I need some time to grow into that name."

The King stepped forward. "Steadfast will stay in the Castle with me for a while, reading the Great Book and exploring. That way, he will grow stronger, and learn to overcome the obstacles he will face..."

"Before they overcome me!" Steadfast nodded. "I need to learn to be a good husband and a good father. I can't do it by myself."

Moira and Seeker were disappointed, but they understood. "OK, Dad! We'll know right where to find you!"

"A feast has been prepared in the ship's dining hall to welcome Steadfast back to my Kingdom!" the King announced, taking Gladness by the hand. "Let's go and celebrate with Gladness! After all, it was Gladness who helped you all defeat the storm of Sadness!"

Gladness was amazed, "How did you know about that, King? You weren't even here during the storm!"

"*Really?*" asked the King, with his eyebrows raised and a smile playing at the corners of his mouth.

Everyone excitedly climbed down to the lower room of the ship. Sure enough, the dining hall had somehow been transformed into a huge banqueting room. There was steaming hot food, music, and lots of fun waiting for them.

Toward the end of the meal, while the minstrels played songs of the Kingdom, the King turned quietly to Seeker. He leaned forward, smiled one of his mysterious smiles, and winked, motioning for Seeker to follow him. Everyone was so busy talking and singing that they didn't notice the two of them slip up the stairs to the deck of the ship.

The sun was just starting to go down, and the sky was full of beautiful colors. In the distance were the shores of the Kingdom. Seeker was sure that he could see his mother standing there, waving.

He waved back and turned excitedly to the King. "Wow! We sure have a surprise for her, don't we King!"

"We sure do," agreed the King. "Oh, and Seeker, I want to give you something."

The King reached inside a pocket of his royal robe and pulled out...Seeker's model ship, perfectly mended and restored.

"Always remember, Seeker—I can put *anything* together that's been broken."

Think About the Story

When bad things happen in our lives...in our families... the King wants to help us. He loves to fix things that are broken—especially broken hearts. Sometimes life can't be put back together like it used to be, but King Jesus certainly can put our hearts back together! He can make them even stronger than they were before the problem!

Despair is not a good place to live. If you ever find yourself there, get out! King Jesus is the Answer. Kneel before Him and any dragons—Discouragement, Bitterness, Fear, Anger, or Greed—will lose their power over you.

Talk to the King

"Hi, King Jesus. Today I give you any broken pieces that are in my heart. I choose to trust You. I choose to sing to my Sadness, and I command the Winds of Weariness to stop blowing in my life. I refuse to live in Despair. I believe that You are the Way, the Truth, and the Life. You are the Answer. Thank You, King Jesus. Thank You."

Read from the King's Great Book—Psalm 42

I speak to the sadness in my heart—
"Hey, heart! You believe!"
I'll read some verses from Psalm 42 and
I-WILL-SING! (Great Book Paraphrase)

- **Romans 12:21—Don't let bad stuff overcome you; overcome it!**

- **John 14:6—There is only one Answer.**

- **Romans 12:12—Don't give up.**

- **Psalm 42—Sing to your sadness! (The Psalms are songs!)**

- **Isaiah 61:1-2—There is healing for broken hearts....**

The Dreamer

Chapter One

"The World Beyond the Kingdom," Moira whispered, enjoying the sound of the words. "What a wonderful place it must be!"

The two charming visitors looked at each other knowingly and moved closer to Moira. Fantasy smiled as Trapper spoke with a voice that sounded as smooth as butter, "In the World Beyond the Kingdom," he said softly, "You can go where you want to go, and do what you want to do..."

Fantasy nodded. "And you can be who you want to be!" she said convincingly. "Just think, Moira—a place where you can make all your dreams come true!"

"Really?" Moira responded hopefully, then flipped through the magazines Trapper and Fantasy had given to her. The pages were filled with pictures of shining buildings, tents and balloons, and the smiling faces of all the people who lived in the World Beyond the Kingdom.

Trapper spoke again in his buttery voice, "You will meet Sophistication, Glamor, and Luxury, Moira. I promise. They are good friends of ours. And you will get to know True Happiness."

Fantasy looked at her watch and nodded. "Well, we need to run. We have an appointment with Opportunity right now!"

Moira waved good-bye, tucked the magazines into her school bookbag, and headed back toward her home in the Village of Peace and Harmony. The King's castle sparkled in the sunshine from its place on top of the hill. The Straight and Narrow Path stretched from the castle doors all the way down to the base of the hill and the Big Rock. That rock was a favorite meeting place for Moira's younger brother, Seeker, and his friends.

I hope Seeker isn't there today, Moira thought to herself. *I need to get home without having to answer any of his questions. Why should it matter to Seeker what I do with my time, anyway? I know I'm not allowed outside the Kingdom borders; and I didn't go outside of them...I just went to the edge! I didn't do anything wrong!*

Moira crossed the bridge into the Kingdom and was relieved to see that no one was at the Big Rock. She quickly turned toward the Village of Peace and Harmony. Maybe, just maybe, she would be lucky enough to get home before anyone noticed her.

Moira didn't realize that someone *had* noticed her. Seeker and some of his friends had watched her whole conversation with Trapper and Fantasy. As soon as Moira was out of hearing distance, Seeker, KnowSo, and Glee peeked out from behind the Big Rock. Then Dawdle and Slow peered out from behind them.

"See? I told you," Seeker said, shaking his head and sitting down on the rock.

"No wonder she hasn't been coming to the Adventure Club meetings lately," KnowSo said. "All the reasons she gave...I bet none of them were true..."

Glee sat on the rock beside Seeker. She was very upset. "I didn't believe you, Seeker," she whispered. "I still can hardly believe this is happening."

"Wh-Wh-Why wo-wo-would Moira g-g-go out there?" Dawdle and Slow asked together.

"That's what I'd like to know," Seeker said. "I'd also like to know the names of the people she was talking to. I've been thinking that maybe I should just go find them and tell them to leave my sister alone!"

KnowSo shook his head. "No—never do that, Seeker. I *know* who they are."

"You do?" Seeker and Glee asked together.

KnowSo nodded. "I was reading about them in the King's library just last week. Their names are Trapper and Fantasy. They've been around for a very long time. Every day they walk near the Kingdom borders looking for children who are almost grown-up; people right around Moira's age."

"Why?" Seeker asked, his heart beating faster.

"They tell them lies about how much fun it would be to live in the World Beyond the Kingdom. They make the lies sound like the truth."

"M-M-Moira needs our help!" Dawdle said.

Slow nodded. "Wh-Wh-What can we do?" she asked.

"Should we tell the other kids?" KnowSo asked. "After all, Moira is a leader of the Adventure Club. The kids should know..."

Seeker shook his head. "Let's wait. I'll try talking to her tonight."

Chapter Two

When Moira reached home, she took a deep breath and quietly opened the door...

"Moira, is that you?" her mother, Contentment, called out.

"Yeah, it's me," Moira answered, disappointed.

Contentment came around the corner with her gardening gloves on and dirt smudged across her face. "You're home rather late today, aren't you?" she asked. Moira shrugged, and Contentment pressed her a bit more. "Did you have a meeting after school?" she asked.

"Yeah, a meeting," Moira answered. "Now I have homework to do."

"Do you have time to help me plant some new flowers?"

"Sorry, Mom," Moira said abruptly, going into her room.

Contentment stood looking at Moira's closed door and felt concern welling up in her heart. What was wrong with Moira? *It's not the door to her room that worries me,* Contentment thought. *The door to her heart seems to be closing as well.*

Alone in her room, Moira threw her bookbag on her bed angrily. *Flowers! She wants me to plant flowers? Doesn't she know I have more important things to think about? More important things to dream about!*

Moira shut her eyes and began to hum her favorite song. It was a song she herself had written. She had never sung it for anyone else; she just kept the words and music close to herself, and every day Moira would sing the song and dance around her room, dreaming of the future—where she would go, what she would do, and who she would be.

> *Hold a dream in your heart;*
> *Hold a castle, hold a rainbow*
> *Hold a picture, hold a promise, hold a prayer.*
> *For everything has a beginning;*
> *Mighty trees come from little seeds...*
> *And the desire in your heart*
> *for what might be—*
> *Will be—If you'll believe!*
> *So, hold a dream in your heart...*

Moira danced and danced and danced, then sank to the floor and leaned back against her bed. As she flipped through the magazines again, Trapper and Fantasy's words echoed in her mind. "Go where you want to go, do what you want to do, be who you want to be..."

A knock on the door made her jump up in surprise. Quickly, she hid the magazines and opened her school books. "Moira," Seeker called, "can I talk to you?"

"Not right now, Seeker! I'm busy!"

Seeker knocked again, louder this time. "Moira! *Please* can I talk to you?"

Moira angrily stood up and opened the door just wide enough to see her brother's face. "What do you want?" she asked sharply. With a twinge of guilt, she noticed Seeker's hurt expression, but she quickly brushed the feeling aside and spoke sharply again. "Well? What do you want?"

Seeker gulped and took a deep breath. "I want..." he said, "I want to know what is wrong with you lately! What's going on?"

"Nothing!" Moira snapped.

"Something is wrong! I know it is! You hardly ever come with us to the King's Celebration, and when you do come, you hardly eat anything, and you never sing the songs!" Seeker pushed on the door and managed to squeeze through the opening into her room.

"What's it to you? Leave me alone, Seeker!"

"Moira! Don't you remember how you and I went to the Secret Place together and fought the dragons that were holding Dad prisoner? And what about the Adventure Club? Doesn't it matter to you that we all miss you at the meetings?"

Moira felt herself begin to soften, then quickly hardened her heart again. "The Adventure Club is for you little kids! And the King would have gone to get Dad anyway—we didn't have anything to do with that! And we probably just imagined the dragons! Now get out of my room!" Moira pushed her brother into the hallway.

Seeker managed to block the door with his body before Moira had time to close it. "Wait! Moira, please! Talk to me! What's wrong? Maybe I can help..."

Moira's eyes flashed in anger. "How could you help? You're just a kid! And there's nothing wrong, anyway! Just leave me alone!"

This time she managed to slam the door, and Seeker was left standing in the hallway. He leaned close to the door and said, "Moira, if you won't let me help, why not go to the King? He *really* wants to talk to you...I saw him watching you at school the other day! Why not go, just once, and..."

"No!" Moira opened the door unexpectedly, and Seeker nearly fell into the room. "Listen, you can't spend your whole life running to the King about every little thing! There comes a time when a person just has to grow up and make some decisions on their own! That's all I'm doing—making some decisions! Now will you please just leave me alone!" With that she slammed the door again.

"OK, Moira," Seeker whispered through the door. "I'll go now. But whatever is wrong, whatever is making you so upset, I *really* know that the King can help you. Good night."

Moira leaned against the door and waited, listening as Seeker's footsteps went down the hall to his room. She listened to the sound of his door opening and then softly closing.

The ache in her heart felt unbearable. "Seeker's right," she whispered to herself. "There is something wrong with me! Why do I hurt so much inside?"

Moira knew that she should be happy. After all, her father had returned to the Kingdom after being away for so long. The King had rescued him from Despair and changed his name from Wanderer to Steadfast. Lately, Contentment had been visiting Steadfast in the castle where he was living, and they were talking about the possibility of his moving back home again. *I should be so happy!* Moira thought. *Why am I so miserable?*

Moira sat down on the bed beside her school books and thumbed through her math assignment where she had sketched pictures of the World Beyond the Kingdom instead of math equations. It had been so hard to concentrate on school work lately...

In the King's castle was a special tower where the children of the Kingdom went to school. They learned math and science and spelling...and they also learned about the King and his Kingdom. During class time, the King often came to visit the students.

Moira had become more and more uncomfortable when the King came into the classroom. She often looked up from her books to find him watching her. He seemed to be calling to her, "Moira, come and spend some time with me. Moira, let's talk."

In fact, earlier that week, the King had slipped a note into her bag. It was a royal invitation. Sitting there on her bed, Moira opened the envelope and read it again.

Dear Moira,
Please come and talk to me.

Call to me and I will always answer you.
Love forever,
The King

"No!" Moira whispered. "I can't talk to the King! This is my last year in the school. I'm almost grown up now...what if the King has plans for me—what *he* wants me to do, where *he* wants me to go, and who *he* wants me to be, and...what if the King's plans for me are totally different from my dreams?"

Moira shut her eyes tightly as a flood of thoughts raced around in her mind...Trapper and Fantasy's stories, the King's invitation, the words of her song, Seeker's pleading voice... until, totally exhausted, she finally fell asleep. And while she slept, Moira dreamed about the shining buildings in the World Beyond the Kingdom.

Chapter Three

"**H**ow could you help? You're just a kid!"

Moira's sharp words from the night before echoed in Seeker's mind as he awoke the next morning. *Just a kid?* he thought. *Just a kid! Well, around here in the Kingdom, little can be very big! I think it's about time the kids of the Kingdom marched as an army again!*

Seeker jumped out of bed, dressed, ran downstairs, ate some breakfast, and headed toward the door. "Oops! Forgot about my teeth!" Usually Seeker's mother was standing at the door, smiling and holding his toothbrush. But today, Seeker realized the house was strangely quiet.

"Mom?" he called. "Moira? Hey, where is everybody?"

Seeker found his mother in her garden—pulling unusually hard at some weeds that had secured themselves into the ground. She seemed upset, and Seeker hesitated about interrupting her.

"Weeds, Seeker," Contentment spoke, knowing that he was watching her. "We must get rid of the weeds, or they will choke out the good plants and all of these beautiful flowers."

With her eyes brimming with tears, Contentment looked at her son. "Our hearts are like a garden." Tears slipped out and down her cheeks. "Your sister's heart...is like a garden..."

Seeker moved to kneel beside his mother, putting an arm reassuringly around her shoulders. "A flower garden, Mom, just like yours. She'll be OK, you'll see."

Contentment shook her head. "She's gone, Seeker."

Seeker felt like his heart stopped beating. "Gone? What do you mean, gone?"

"Moira left sometime during the night. She left this note for us." Contentment pulled a tear-stained paper from her pocket and read aloud. "Dear Mom and Seeker, you know how hard it's been for me in the Kingdom lately, and I've made my decision. I thought about it a lot and feel like this is what I need to do..."

Contentment's voice broke and she handed the note to Seeker to continue reading. "I'm not sure where I'm going except that I'm going to make my dreams come true. Please don't try to find me. I'll write you a letter when I get settled. I still love you, and I'm sorry that I have to do this. Moira."

Seeker stood up, determination filling his heart. "The King will know what to do, Mom! He will go and get Moira and bring her home, I just know it! I'm going for help!"

Seeker hurried through the gate and raced through the streets of Peace and Harmony, calling to his friends, "Emergency meeting in the King's Throne Room! Right away!" he shouted as he ran past their homes.

HopeSo, KnowSo, and Yes; Giggles, Gladness, and Glee; Doodle and Do hurried out of their houses and followed close behind Seeker. Dawdle and Slow struggled to keep up. "Wh-wh-what's wrong, Seeker?" Dawdle called.

"I-I-Is M-M-Moira OK, Seeker?" Slow asked, running as fast as her legs would carry her.

With panting sentences, Seeker explained about Moira's note as he led his friends past the Big Rock and up the Straight and Narrow Path to the castle.

The Doorkeeper didn't stop the children with his usual question, "Do you *really* want to see the King?" Instead, he quickly opened the door just in time for the army of children to race through. They slid down the shining hallway—not for fun today, but just because it was faster than walking—and flung themselves through the door of the Throne Room.

The King was standing there, as though he had been expecting them.

"King, King!" Seeker cried out. "Moira left the Kingdom!"

"I *know,*" the King said quietly.

"She was gone when Mom and I got up this morning!" Seeker hurried on, not aware that the King had answered him.

"I *know,*" the King repeated.

Finally, Seeker realized what the King had said. "You *know?*" he exclaimed, "Then why don't you do something! King, you have to go and get her!"

The King quietly shook his head. "No, Seeker, not until she *really* wants me to. Come, let's go out to the courtyard."

As they walked outside, Glee pleaded with the King, "Please, King! We love Moira!"

"Yes!" Yes agreed, taking the King's hand. "We *really* love her! Please go and get her!"

"D-D-Don't worry," Dawdle said reassuringly. "The K-K-King will l-l-look after Moira."

Slow looked up at the King, her eyes wide with trust, and said, "W-W-Won't you, King!"

Seeker was frantic. "King! You just have to go and get her and make her come back!"

The King shook his head. "No. Not until she *really* wants me to." The King smiled gently at Seeker and his friends. "But there is something that all of you can do for Moira...something that will *really* help her."

"What, King?" the children asked hopefully.

"Spend time in the Secret Place. Talk to me every day about Moira."

(The Secret Place is a special place where people can go and talk to the King about how they feel. They don't always see him, but he is always there.)

"OK!" Seeker said. "We'll talk to you in the Secret Place. And what about us marching as an army, King? Like when we defeated the dragon Greed!"

"Yeah, let's *do* it!" Doodle said enthusiastically. "We can be your army again, King! We can go and rescue Moira from... from..." he paused, seeing Seeker's horrified expression.

"Dragons," Seeker whispered. "I never even thought about dragons! King! Are there dragons after Moira?"

The King put his arm around Seeker's shoulders to comfort him. "Dragons sent messengers to speak to Moira, and she listened to their voices."

"Trapper and Fantasy," KnowSo nodded knowingly.

"But no dragons will be able to touch Moira if you stand guard," the King said, looking at the anxious young faces around him. "In the Secret Place, you can be my army, my very big little army. Moira will be protected." The King paused for a moment, then continued, "I will be watching her. The moment she calls to me, I will answer her!"

"OK, King," Seeker said, and his friends nodded their agreement. "We will spend time every day in the Secret Place!"

"We will *do* it!" Doodle and Do announced together.

Chapter Four

Weeks and months passed, and whenever Seeker wasn't with his friends in the Secret Place, he spent time helping Contentment in her flower garden. On one such day, Seeker took a deep breath and said, "Mom, this place smells so good! I just love coming here!"

Contentment smiled and sat down, wiping her brow with a happy sigh. "It is nice, isn't it? It's my Secret Place..."

"Your Secret Place?" echoed Seeker.

"Yes. I love talking with the King while I work in this garden. It helps me to remember that the garden he is most interested in is right in here." Contentment pointed to her heart.

"My Secret Place is in one of the towers of the castle," Seeker said, as he sat down beside Contentment. "My friends and I have been going there every day to talk to the King about Moira. He said that if we would do that, she would be protected."

"Yes," Contentment nodded. "And as I talk to the King here in my garden, I sometimes feel as though I am working in the garden of Moira's heart. I'm planting good seeds...and someday soon, those seeds will prove stronger than the weeds that Moira allowed to grow."

"Weeds," Seeker said thoughtfully. "Is that why she left the Kingdom, Mom? What kind of weeds?"

"I've tried to name some of them as I pull weeds out of this garden," Contentment said. "I think the main weeds in Moira's heart were Guilt, Anger, and Silence."

Seeing Seeker's wondering expression, Contentment continued, "I think the weeds entered Moira's heart around the time

171

your father became Wanderer and lived in Despair. Moira felt guilty because she thought that somehow she should have been able to stop your dad from leaving us."

"That's not true!" Seeker exclaimed. "Dad made that choice— Moira had nothing to do with it! That's a lie!"

"Believing lies is how the weeds begin, Seeker," Contentment explained. "Then Moira allowed Anger to creep into her heart. She kept silent about how she was really feeling...and that Silence made it easier for the weeds to take root."

"Silence...She never talked to you?" asked Seeker.

"She didn't talk to me," Contentment answered, "and I'm fairly certain that she didn't talk to the King, either. I mean *really* talk to him—you know, about how she was feeling inside."

Suddenly, Seeker sat up straight and exclaimed, "Oh no! I just remembered something that happened back when the Adventure Club first began! We all went with the King to the underground passageway between Royal Harbor and the castle. The King was teaching us about not living in Darkness; and that day he asked Moira to come and talk to him about how she was really feeling..."

"And did she do that?" Contentment asked.

Seeker shook his head. "I don't think so. She and I began to go to my Secret Place together, and we talked to the King about Dad...but I don't think that Moira ever had a Secret Place of her own.... No wonder the King looked so worried about her that day!"

Contentment sighed. "She seemed to be close to the King.... I just assumed that she was talking to him about her feelings. It's so important to do that!" Contentment reached inside her apron pocket where she always carried a copy of the King's Great Book. "Here, Seeker, let me show you something...." She flipped through the pages until she came to the place she was looking for.

"Pour out your heart to the King," she read aloud. "He is a very present help in times of trouble." Contentment closed the book and held it to her heart. "If Moira would have poured out her feelings to the King, those feelings would have been healed..."

"And the weeds would have been pulled out of her garden before they really took root," Seeker said.

Contentment stood up and said, "During the past few days as I've worked, a new song has been growing in my heart, Seeker. Would you like to hear it?"

Seeker nodded quickly. His mom was great at making up songs! She sang it through once, then Seeker joined in. The song was so much fun that Contentment and Seeker danced around the garden with a hoe and rake as they sang...

My heart is a garden
Where the King goes walkin'
And I want him to like it here...
I want the trees and the flowers
To really overpower
Any little weeds—like fear....
I will pull out things like worry or anger
Before they have a chance to take root
I'll plant seeds like kindness and forgiveness
And watch my garden grow fruit!

I won't listen to lies—that always seem to try
To take my attention from the truth!
And if my heart becomes hard—
turning from light to the dark
Then this—is what I'll do:

I will run to the King and I'll
pour out my troubles
I will tell him my worries and fears

Yes I will run to the King, and I
will clean out my garden

'Cause I want him to like it here...

"Wonderful!" said the King as he clapped and smiled from the entrance of the flower garden.

Contentment and Seeker turned toward him and bowed low in delighted surprise. "Your Majesty!"

Seeker ran to hug him. "Hi, King!"

The King smiled a bigger smile and said, "Hi." Then he reached out his hands to Seeker and Contentment. "Come," said the King, "I will show you what happened in this garden while you sang!"

Contentment and Seeker looked at each other, wondering. What could have happened while they sang? They walked with the King to the far corner of the flower garden. There, beside a strong fruit tree, was a fountain. It was bubbling with crystal clear water that flowed out into a sparkling little pond.

"Wow!" said Seeker. "Where did that come from?"

"From my castle," said the King. "The water in that fountain is the same water that flows out from my throne room..."

"It's beautiful, King!" Contentment said as she hugged him. "Thank you!"

Seeker watched his mother with a new sense of appreciation. All that she has been through, Seeker thought to himself, all the problems with Dad...and now the problems with Moira.... But Mom just keeps spending time here in her Secret Place, and no weeds like anger or worry can grow inside her.

Seeker leaned against a rock near the fountain, and his thoughts again turned toward his sister. If only Moira would find a Secret Place and talk to the King...

Chapter Five

"I t's b-b-been a v-v-very long time since M-M-Moira l-left the Kingdom," Dawdle said one day as the children met together in the Secret Place.

The others nodded and turned away from the Window of the Secret Place, feeling discouraged. No pictures had been seen through the Window for a long time.

"H-H-Have you h-h-heard any thing from her, S-S-Seeker?" asked Slow, "A-Anything at all?"

Seeker shook his head. "No. Not one word. All this waiting is so hard! I've been wondering if there isn't something we could be doing to help Moira."

Doodle and Do agreed excitedly. "Great idea! Let's *do* something!"

"Yes!" Yes exclaimed. "I mean, after all, we *are* the King's army! There must be something we can do to help Moira!"

The other children stood at attention and saluted. They were the King's army! Ready for battle!

KnowSo shook his head and motioned for them to relax. "You *know* we can't do anything until the King gives the orders," he said.

"OK, OK," said Seeker with a sigh. Glee had been quietly looking through the Window of the Secret Place while her friends talked; but now she exclaimed, "I just saw a picture!"

"A picture?" Giggles echoed as everyone gathered around Glee. "What was it?" The children peered through the Window intently, but no one could see a picture except Glee.

"A map!" she exclaimed. "Yes, I think it's a map."

Doodle reached inside his pocket for a pencil and paper. "Tell us what it looks like, and I'll try to draw it!"

Glee peered again through the Window. "OK...I can see the castle...and the bridge. Past that is the World Beyond the Kingdom..."

"The World Beyond the Kingdom?" Seeker echoed excitedly. "That's where Moira is!"

"I *know!*" KnowSo said. "Maybe the King is showing us the exact place where Moira is so that we can go and get her!"

Everyone gathered around Glee. "Look harder," Do said. "What *do* you see now?"

Glee squinted her eyes, struggling to see. Everyone held their breath in anticipation, but then she shook her head. "Sorry. That's all there is."

"M-M-Maybe," Dawdle said, "the m-map isn't for us."

"What do you mean?" the others wanted to know.

"M-M-Maybe the map is for Moira," Dawdle said, "M-M-Maybe she can't find her way back home."

"I know what we'll *do*," cried Do excitedly. "Doodle can draw a map for Moira, and we'll send it to her!"

The others stared at Do with blank expressions. "D-D-Do you have her address?" Slow asked.

"Oh, uh, well, no," stuttered Do. "I guess that was a really dumb idea, huh?"

Seeker came to his friend's rescue. "No, it was a great idea!"

"*Do* you really think so?" Do asked hopefully.

"Yes!" Seeker said. "Listen, we can send the map to Moira—we can ask the King to take it to her!"

"How?"

"In a dream," Seeker said intensely. "Moira was always talking about her dreams! Let's ask the King to send her a dream—a dream that would help her find her way back home!"

"OK!" shouted Do. "Let's *do* it!"

As the children joined hands in the Secret Place, Seeker shut his eyes tightly and whispered, "Wherever she is right now...send her a dream, King. Help Moira find her way back home."

"Y-Y-Yes, King," said Dawdle and Slow, "and wh-wh-wherever she is, please protect her..."

Chapter Six

"**H**elp! Please someone, help me!"

The voice of a young woman cried out from a dark alley, and a moment later she was thrown down some worn steps where she landed in a pool of mud. Two men stood in the doorway.

"That'll teach you!" one man roared. The second man angrily pointed his finger at her. "Who do you think you are, anyway? Now get out of here before we really hurt you!"

The young woman struggled to her feet and pushed her matted hair away from her eyes.

It was Moira.

Trembling from the close call she had just had with Rage and Jealousy, Moira wrapped her coat around her thin body and hurried down the alley. "Whew," she whispered. "They were just about to strike me when for some reason they stopped! That was scary."

When she reached a dimly lit street, Moira paused to rest. Some of Jealousy's words echoed in her mind. "Who do you think you are, anyway?" Over and over again the phrase repeated, "Who do you think you are, anyway?"

That's a very good question, Moira thought. *Who am I?* As Moira sat there, the deepest longings of her heart took the shape of a song, and she sang it softly...

Who am I? Why am I?
Where am I going?
Won't someone show me the way?

Who am I? Why am I?
Where am I going?
Won't someone show me the way?
I used to have a dream inside of my heart—
A vision and a promise filled with hope...
But now those dreams and visions
They've all shattered
And nothing seems to matter anymore.
How I used to dream
Of the person I would be.
How I used to dream of the people
I would meet.
How I used to...dream...

Suddenly, Moira realized that someone was watching her, listening to her song. A tall, slender woman moved quietly across the street and stood beside Moira.

"Who are you?" Moira whispered.

"My name is Loneliness," came the soft reply. "I heard you singing. You sounded like you needed a friend. Can I walk with you for a while?"

Moira smiled and nodded, "Thanks, yes, I'd like that. I really do need a friend..."

Loneliness seemed right at home in the dark pathways Moira chose, and as they walked together, Moira told Loneliness everything that had happened since she had come to live in the World Beyond the Kingdom...

Moira's story was one that Loneliness had heard before, but she listened compassionately as Moira spoke.

For a while, life in the World seemed to be everything Moira had expected it to be. Trapper and Fantasy introduced her to many people. She met Sophistication and made friends with Glamor and Luxury. Although she never got to know True

Happiness, Moira went places, and did things, and felt as though she was on her way to having all her dreams come true.

But...

As the weeks and months passed, Moira discovered that the World Beyond the Kingdom was not what she had expected it to be, after all. The buildings that looked shiny were dull and dreary inside. The life she had dreamed about did not exist. The farther she got from the Kingdom, the darker it became, and the people Moira had thought were her friends were not her friends after all.

Trapper and Fantasy moved away to a different city without telling Moira where they went.

Glamor became Emptiness. Luxury became Poverty, and Moira learned that Sophistication's real name was Charade.

For a few short weeks, Moira had thought she had met True Happiness, but then discovered that the person was wearing a mask and was actually Rage. That's who had thrown her out onto the street a few hours earlier.

As Moira finished telling Loneliness her story, she shivered again with a mixture of fear and relief. "Rage and Jealousy were about to strike me. They were so angry! But then, for some reason, they just threw me out of the door!"

"Someone was watching out for you," Loneliness said softly.

Moira was startled. "Someone was watching out for me?" she repeated. "But no one even knows where I am! And no one would care, anyway." An uncomfortable ache came into Moira's heart and she tried to ignore it.

"So, Loneliness," she said, "what about you? Tell me about yourself."

But Loneliness didn't answer. She just pulled her coat closer to her face for warmth and they kept walking.

Chapter Seven

More time went by while Moira explored the World Beyond the Kingdom, still hoping that somehow all of her dreams would happen. But the farther she got from the Kingdom, the darker her life became. Several times, Moira was sure that she had seen dragons peering out from their hiding places along her path; but she continued on, hoping that around the next corner she might meet Opportunity, or perhaps she might still find True Happiness, as Trapper and Fantasy had promised.

But after months and months of searching, Moira found herself in a sad and miserable place called "The Valley of Lost Dreams" with Loneliness as her constant companion. The only sound was the distant bleating of sheep in a pasture.

Much of the time Moira and Loneliness spent together was spent in silence, each thinking their own troubled, lonely thoughts. Although Loneliness rarely spoke, Moira learned that she had a young son. The few times Loneliness mentioned him, her eyes filled with sorrow and she would whisper, "So many regrets. So many regrets..." Then she would grow silent again and refuse to answer Moira's questions.

One morning, Moira said to Loneliness, "I had a dream last night."

Loneliness turned to her with interest. Dreams were very, very rare in that valley.

"I dreamed I was lost in a garden," Moira said.

Loneliness came and sat closer, and Moira continued, "It was very dark and the garden was overgrown with weeds. The harder I tried to find my way out, the more lost I became, and I got tangled up in the weeds." Moira shivered remembering.

"And then what happened?" Loneliness asked.

"My brother, Seeker...he came to me in the garden and handed me a map...At least, I thought it was a map; but then, when I looked at it, it was actually the words of a song."

Moira stood up, suddenly excited as she remembered more details of the dream. "Yes, it was a song, but not just any song! It was a song that I myself wrote a very long time ago. I had forgotten all about it! The words are: Hold a dream in your heart..." Moira paused, then remembered more of the words. "Hold a castle, hold a rainbow...Hold a picture, hold a promise, hold a prayer..."

The words bubbled up inside Moira and although she couldn't remember the melody, she began to dance around just like she used to dance in her room at night...

After a few moments of dancing and struggling to bring the music back to her mind, Moira became aware that Loneliness was watching her with a look of deep pity.

"You don't believe me!" Moira said in surprise as she stopped dancing. "You think I'm just making it all up, don't you?"

Loneliness shook her head but Moira continued, "Well it's true! I did have dreams! Lots and lots of wonderful dreams!"

Loneliness again looked at Moira with deep pity. "I'm so sorry," she whispered. "I'm so sorry you've lost your dreams, Moira. I'm so sorry you've forgotten the music of your song. Maybe if you tried again to remember...maybe if you thought some more about the dream that you had last night..."

Moira nodded and smiled feebly at Loneliness. "OK. I'll try."

She shut her eyes and thought again about the paper Seeker had handed to her in the dream. Suddenly, Moira could see it just as clearly as when she dreamed it...but now, the paper no longer held the words of a song. Instead, on the paper was a picture of the

King...and there, beneath his picture, were the words of the invitation he had given to her so long ago.

Moira's eyes shot open, and she stood up so suddenly that Loneliness was startled. It had been such a long time since Moira had thought about the King. The expression on his face in the picture was exactly the same as when he used to look at her. "I wonder what he wanted to say to me?" she asked aloud.

"Who?" asked Loneliness.

"Someone I used to know," answered Moira. "Someone very wonderful. He wanted me to come and talk to him, but...but I was afraid."

Loneliness nodded. "Fear keeps people from doing what they later wish they would have done; or else it makes them do things they wish they would not have done." Loneliness' voice dropped to a whisper and her eyes filled with deep sorrow. "Regrets. So many regrets..."

Moira took hold of her friend's hands and spoke earnestly. "I wish I would have gone to see him...just once...just once! Why didn't I do that?" Moira's voice trailed off and she dropped Loneliness' hands. "Oh well, it's too late now. He's probably really angry with me for leaving the Kingdom, and even if I wanted to go back, it's too far. I'd never find my way."

"The Kingdom?" asked Loneliness. "You were in a Kingdom?" When Moira nodded, Loneliness spoke hopefully. "And a King... is there really a King? I heard about him once but...is he real?"

Moira nodded again, and dug through her bag, searching. "Here it is—the King's invitation! I could never bring myself to throw it away." She handed it to Loneliness, who opened the envelope carefully and read aloud:

Dear Moira,
Please come and talk to me.
Call to me and I will always answer you.

Love forever,
The King

Loneliness looked up, her eyes wide. "An invitation from the King. A personal letter from him! Oh, Moira..."

Tears welled up in Moira's eyes, and she nodded. "Yes. A personal invitation from the King, and I ignored it!" She wiped the tears away and then continued with an intensity Loneliness had never heard before. "If I had the chance, I would do things differently. I never would have left the Kingdom! I promise I would have stayed there! If only the King would give me another chance. If only it wasn't too late!"

At that very moment, Moira heard a sound. She looked up. There, in the meadow across from the Valley of Lost Dreams, was a lamb. It was the saddest looking little lamb that Moira had ever seen. It was struggling through the grass, tripping, falling, and crying out in pain and confusion.

"Oh, the poor thing!" Moira exclaimed to Loneliness. "It must have gotten out from the pasture somehow! I wonder what we can do to help it?"

But before either Moira or Loneliness could think of a way to help the lamb, a shepherd came. He stepped out from the thick forest near the Valley of Lost Dreams and walked over to where the crumpled little heap of wool had fallen. The shepherd bent down and gently picked up the lamb in his strong arms, and holding it very closely, carried it away.

Tears spilled out and over Moira's cheeks as she watched. "That's me," she whispered. "That's me! I'm just like that lamb! Oh, Loneliness, I'm so lost and so scared and oh, I really wish I had a second chance!" Moira fell down to her knees, crying.

Loneliness gently touched Moira's shoulder and pointed. There, coming toward them, was the shepherd. He walked swiftly and purposefully, as though he had something important to do.

Moira quickly wiped the tears away. They weren't used to visitors coming to the Valley. "I wonder what he wants," she said.

"Perhaps," Loneliness whispered to Moira with a tender
smile, "perhaps he is looking for another lost lamb."

Loneliness shyly stepped back as the shepherd approached.
He stood silently for a moment in front of Moira, and then, very
slowly, the shepherd pushed back the hood of his cloak.

It was...the King.

Moira gasped with surprise. The King! What was he doing
here in the Valley of Lost Dreams? What did he think of her being
in such a place? Shame and embarrassment washed through
Moira like a wave. She bowed her head low and turned away,
silently asking the King to leave her. But the King did not leave.
Instead, he bent down to the place where Moira was, gently
picked her up in his strong arms, and held her closely, just like
he had held the little lamb. And then, ever so softly, the King
began to sing...

> *Hold a dream in your heart*
> *Hold a castle, hold a rainbow*
> *Hold a picture, Hold a promise*
> *Hold a prayer...*

Moira was amazed. "King! King, that's the song I used to sing!
I was trying to remember the tune...!" Moira broke off, suddenly
confused. "But...I wrote that song! Where did you learn it?"

The King held her even closer. "Moira," he whispered gently,
"I was the one who put the song in your heart!"

Then the King began to tell Moira about the dreams he had
for her life—where he wanted her to go, what he wanted her to
do, and who he wanted her to be.

And they were her dreams!

"My dreams," she whispered, as they poured back into her
heart like a flood. Cheerful dreams, big dreams, plans and

visions for the future tumbled through her mind one after the other like a joyful parade. "My dreams are back! But now they are brighter and even more wonderful than before!"

Moira shut her eyes tightly, watching the happy thoughts in her mind. As she watched, she saw some of the dream from the night before. She was in a garden, but the tangled weeds were gone. Flowering plants, just beginning to bud, lined a pathway. In the center of the garden was a golden bench, and on the bench sat the King. His expression was the same one she had seen so many times before. He was calling to her, "Come and talk to me. Call to me, and I will always answer you..."

Moira's eyes shot open in realization. She knew what it was he wanted to talk to her about...it was her future! The King wanted to talk to her about the dreams that he himself had placed in her heart. She had never needed to fear the King's plans for her; what she needed to do was to get close to him!

The King smiled at Moira, seeing the light of understanding in her eyes. He stood to his feet, still holding her in his great arms. "Let's go home," he said.

As they headed back toward the Kingdom, away from the Valley of Lost Dreams, Moira nestled deeper into the King's arms. *He's not angry!* she thought. *He came all this way just to get me; he has plans, dreams for my life—dreams that now seem even more wonderful than before!*

Love for the King welled up inside her heart like a garden of flowers ready to burst into bloom. Moira impulsively threw her arms around the King's neck and hugged him really tight.

The King laughed...and his laughter filled the whole valley....

Back in the Kingdom, Seeker and his friends had been watching through the Window of the Secret Place.

"Hooray!" everyone shouted as they hugged Seeker. "Moira's coming home! Moira's coming home!"

After a few moments of happy celebrating, the children hurried out from the Secret Place and raced down the Straight and Narrow Path toward the Big Rock. They wanted to be there when the King and Moira arrived.

"I'll be right back," Seeker shouted. "I'm going to get Mom!"

None of the children noticed that two of their friends weren't with them. They didn't realize that Dawdle and Slow were still looking through the Window, tears falling silently down their cheeks. "I-I'm happy for M-Moira," Dawdle said.

"B-But what about L-L-Loneliness?" asked Slow.

Dawdle and Slow watched Loneliness huddled on a bench and shivering in the cool air; and they watched the King. Just before he and Moira left the Valley of Lost Dreams, the King turned back toward the lonely young woman. He looked at her intently and smiled a mysterious smile. Then the King looked directly through the Window of the Secret Place, right at Dawdle and Slow. He leaned forward slightly and winked at them.

A wave of delighted relief washed through the two children. "Th-The King has a pl-pl-plan for L-Loneliness!" Dawdle cried excitedly.

Slow nodded happily. "H-He's not going to l-l-leave her in Lost Dreams!"

And then Dawdle and Slow hurried from the Secret Place as fast as they were able. They wanted to be there to welcome Moira back to the Kingdom of Joy and Peace.

Think About the Story

Perhaps you have wonderful dreams in your heart about the future. Jesus Christ is the King of all kings. He has dreams for your life. Have you ever asked Him what they are? Or perhaps you used to know His dreams, but you've been wandering away. If you are in the Valley of Lost Dreams, call out to the King! He will pick you up, heal your wounds, and make the dreams in your heart new again.

Talk to the King

"Hi, King. Sometimes people ask me what
I'm going to do when I grow up. I need to ask
You that question! There are lots and lots of
things I can plan and think about doing. Please
help me to spend my time seeking You about
my future. The world beyond Your Kingdom
looks attractive, but I know that the dreams
that You put into my heart will only come true
as I stay in Your Kingdom, close to You."

Read from the King's Great Book—Ephesians 3:20

The King is able to do—
Exceeding, abundantly—

Above all I ask or think—
According to His power in me!
Ephesians chapter 3 and verse 20—
Dream big dreams, everybody!
(Great Book Paraphrase)

- **Jeremiah 29:11—His plans for you are GOOD**

- **Proverbs 16:25—Careful! There is a path that looks right, but it's not!**

- **Proverbs 29:18—Don't live carelessly**

Armor of Light

Chapter One

Seeker knocked again. "Please, Moira, can I come in? Just for a few minutes?"

There was no response; so he knocked another time. "Moira, I *really* want to talk to you! Please?"

Seeker heard Moira sigh a deep sigh, "Oh...all right."

Seeker walked in, and there was his sister. Her eyes were red and puffy, and soggy tissues were scattered all over the bed. Seeker found a place among the tissues and sat down. "Moira, what's wrong? What's the matter? Ever since you came back to the Kingdom you've been so sad! And I thought you would be happy! I was looking forward to all the adventures we would go on together."

Moira turned her puffy eyes toward him and said with a sob, "Oh, Seeker, I can't forget them!"

"Forget who?"

"I can't forget all the people I met when I lived in the World Beyond the Kingdom! Oh, Seeker, it's awful out there. It's so dark, and so empty; and I'm sure that I saw some dragons hiding throughout the streets and alleys. Ugh! It was as if those horrible creatures were just waiting for their chance to grab people! The people...the people don't know about the King, Seeker. They don't even know that there's a Kingdom!"

"I keep thinking and thinking about them; I remember their faces, and I just hurt inside. Especially this one friend I had—her name was Loneliness. She told me once that she had a son—but whenever I asked about him, she would whisper, 'So many regrets. So many regrets...' Isn't that sad, Seeker? And I don't even know what his name was."

Moira paused for a moment to blow her nose, then continued. "Loneliness was with me in the Valley of Lost Dreams when the King found me...and I just left her there! How could I do that? Why didn't I ask her to come to the Kingdom with me?"

Moira sighed another deep sigh. "Anyway, I remember Loneliness, and I remember all the other people and Seeker, I just hurt inside."

"Moira, what you need is a Secret Place!"

"A Secret Place?" she echoed.

"Yeah, a Secret Place," said Seeker. "Don't you remember how you and I used to go there together? Don't you remember how we fought the dragons that were holding Dad in chains?!"

Moira nodded slowly. "That all seems so long ago, Seeker, but I do remember."

"Well, I have a Secret Place in one of the towers of the Castle; and I'm the only one who has the key to that room. I can go there any time I want, and the King is always there. I don't always see him, but he is always there." Seeker moved closer to his sister and put an arm around her shoulders. "If you go to your Secret Place, Moira, you can tell the King how much you hurt inside, and he'll tell you what to do."

"Oh Seeker," Moira said as she blew her nose again, "that's a great idea. I've stayed in here crying, but I haven't cried out to the *King!* I'm going to find my own special Secret Place right now!"

Moira stood to her feet and walked toward the door; then

she paused and turned back. "Thanks, little brother," she said, and gave Seeker a warm hug.

"You're welcome, Moira."

After Moira had gone, Seeker continued to sit quietly in her room, thinking. *Hmm...I guess there are lots of people out there who don't know about the King...and there are probably more dragons, too! I think I should go to the...*

Just then Seeker's mother, Contentment, called, "Seeker, will you come and help me, please?"

"Sure, Mom!" he answered. "Where are you?"

"The stairs to the attic!" she called. "Hurry!"

The attic was a little room at the very top of their house where Seeker's mother kept boxes of things that the family didn't need or use very often. When Seeker reached her, Contentment was halfway up and halfway down the stairs to the attic—with a bed! Seeker pushed on the bed and helped her to get it up the stairway.

Seeker looked around the attic room in surprise. Instead of boxes, there was a chest of drawers, a night table, and a lamp in the room. "Mom, what are you doing up here?"

"I'm changing this into a bedroom," she replied.

"Why?" asked Seeker.

"I don't know!" his mother answered.

"You don't know?!" he echoed.

Contentment shrugged her shoulders as she made the bed up with a fluffy warm comforter. "The King just told me to get it ready, so I am."

"This is great, Mom!" Seeker said, looking around at the cozy little room. "I wonder what the King has in mind. Didn't he even give you a hint?"

"No. He just told me to get it ready; and I've learned how much fun it is to trust him when he tells me to do something—

especially when I don't understand why." Contentment smiled at Seeker and winked. "It's an adventure!"

"An adventure," Seeker nodded. "Mom, I just was on my way to the Secret Place when you called me. I'd better go now. See you later!"

Chapter Two

When Seeker reached the Big Rock at the base of the Straight and Narrow Path, he was surprised to see his friends there: HopeSo, KnowSo, and Yes; Giggles, Gladness, and Glee; Doodle and Do...and they were all crowded around Dawdle and Slow.

"D-D-Don't w-w-worry about us," Dawdle was saying. "W-W-We'll be OK."

Seeker hurried over. "Dawdle and Slow! What happened?"

"Bullies," KnowSo explained. "Some kids have been picking on Dawdle and Slow again."

Seeker sighed and shook his head. Dawdle and Slow were different than most children. They talked and walked very, very slowly. Seeker and his friends had come to admire Dawdle and Slow because they were wise and cautious and took time to care about other people. But children who didn't know them often made fun of Dawdle and Slow and said very cruel words to them.

"I'm on my way up to my Secret Place," Seeker said. "Why don't you all come with me and we'll talk to the King. He will help Dawdle and Slow!"

"I *hope* so!" said HopeSo.

"I *know* so!" agreed KnowSo.

"Yes, yes, of course he will!" Yes said with confidence.

The children greeted the Doorkeeper and then slid down the shining hallway. They all followed Seeker up the winding stairs to a room in one of the Castle's high towers. Seeker unlocked the door of his Secret Place. "Come on in everybody," he said.

Hardly a moment later, the door to the Secret Place opened quietly and the children looked up with delighted surprise. "King! You're here!" Giggles laughed happily.

"He's always here," KnowSo explained knowingly, "We just don't always see him."

The King smiled and said, "Hi" in his deep kingly voice. "Hi, King," the children responded.

"I came to talk to you about Moira, King," Seeker began. "She's really sad because of people living in the World Beyond the Kingdom."

The King nodded. "I *know,*" he said.

"And I began feeling sad myself," Seeker continued. "I got to wondering how many people are out there who don't know you...they must feel sad, too."

"Speaking of sad," KnowSo interrupted, "we know some people right here who are sad!"

The children made way so that Dawdle and Slow could be next to the King. "M-M-My heart hurts, King," Dawdle said.

"M-M-Mine t-t-too," Slow nodded her agreement.

"I *know,*" the King responded as he pulled Dawdle and Slow close to himself. "Here, let me touch your hearts." The King very gently touched Dawdle and Slow's hearts and they smiled.

"Th-th-thanks, King," Dawdle smiled.

Slow looked surprised. "W-W-Wow! I st-st-still remember the w-w-words that those kids said, b-b-but it d-d-doesn't hurt nearly as much anymore!"

Seeker closely watched the King with Dawdle and Slow. *If only all the people out in the World Beyond the Kingdom could get to know the King,* he thought.

The King looked directly at Seeker, leaned forward, and winked. Then he reached out his hands to the children. "Come. I want to show you something."

The King led the children over to the Window of the Secret

Place, where the King shows his people the way things *really* are, not the way they appear to be. When Seeker and his friends looked out, they saw people. People were everywhere—little people, big people, old people, young people—and they were all busy. Some people were at school, some were working, some were at home, some were playing...

Then suddenly, the picture changed, and the children saw the same people...but now they looked very different. Every single person was blind! And they were all bruised, and crippled, and hurting. Seeker and his friends could hear their cries...and, as they watched, they saw the reason for the people's pain.

Dragons! Hundreds of dragons. Thousands of dragons. All different colors, shapes, and sizes. And every one of them was picking its nose! The children watched with disgust. "That is so gross!" Do exclaimed. "Why do they *do* that, anyway?"

"Oh, I don't believe it!" Glee gasped. "That dragon over there—he blew his nose and didn't even use a tissue!"

"I think I'm going to be sick," Yes said, standing closer to the King.

A nasty odor reached the children's nostrils, and they waved the air, frantically trying to get away from the smell. "Ugh!" cried Glee, holding her nose. "Don't they ever take a bath?"

The dragons were breathing out puffs of incredibly bad breath, sneering, and muttering mean and nasty words. Some dragons wrapped chains around the people and wounded them. Other dragons put their slimy claws over the people's eyes and blinded them with a sort of oozing, slimy screen so the people could still see, but not *really* see...

The King spoke solemnly. "The dragons cripple the people and hurt them," he said. "The dragons keep the people blind so they can't see my Kingdom."

"That's awful!" exclaimed HopeSo.

"That's terrible!" agreed KnowSo.

"Th-th-that's sad," Dawdle and Slow said together.

But as Seeker looked through the Window, he realized that the sadness he had felt earlier had left him. Instead, now he felt *really* upset! Who did those dragons think they were, anyway! Seeker turned to the King and spoke with fierce intensity. "So, what are we going to do about it, King?"

The King smiled at Seeker's courage and put a hand on his shoulder affectionately. "Well, Seeker, do you think you could bring *one* person out of the Darkness, away from the dragons, and into my Kingdom?"

Seeker looked out at the people and again heard their cries, and he looked again at the dragons. Now they seemed even more terrible and disgusting. Seeker gulped, and slowly echoed the King's words. "One person...out of the Darkness...away from the dragons...into your Kingdom..."

The other children looked at Seeker, then at the King, then back through the Window. For long moments they could hardly breathe. This certainly was a different kind of adventure! Seeker hesitated another moment then answered, "OK, King—if you show me which one person, and if you *really* help me!"

"I will help you," said the King. "Look again."

Chapter Three

Seeker and his friends looked through the Window of the Secret Place again and saw that the scene had changed. A young boy about ten years old was standing on a hill not far from the Kingdom. "Decision Hill," the King said, "And beyond it is the Valley of Decision. The boy is called 'NoName,' but he is deciding he doesn't like that name, and his heart is beginning to search...for me."

NoName was walking along the top of the hill like a tough bully, kicking at rocks and saying bad words. His face was dark and cloudy and angry. The King pointed as two ugly, hairy dragons crept toward NoName, "Anger and Abuse," said the King, "Those dragons have power over the boy."

An extremely nasty odor reached the children's nostrils and they again waved the air, frantically trying to get away from the smell. "Ugh!" cried Glee, holding her nose extra tightly, "Those two dragons smell even worse than all the other ones!"

The King nodded. "Anger and Abuse are very, very nasty dragons."

Seeker was watching NoName. "That kid kicking the rocks and using all those bad words and no one is even there to hear him!" Seeker said, "It's like he's just *practicing* being mean."

"H-H-How did that b-b-boy ever get like that, King?" asked Slow.

"Words," the King replied.

"W-W-Words?" Slow echoed questioningly as she glanced at her brother, Dawdle.

The King nodded, "Words can hurt very deeply. And unless you come to me with the pain, the dragons Anger and Abuse will begin to take control. Look at NoName again. You will see some of the reasons why he acts the way he does."

Through the Window of the Secret Place the children were able to see some of NoName's life. They saw him at school and listened as a group of mean children spoke cruel words to him. They saw his embarrassment as a teacher made fun of his failing grade on a test in front of the entire class. And Seeker and his friends watched in dismay as NoName went to his home where his mother said even more cruel words to him and treated him in mean and hurtful ways.

The dragons Anger and Abuse were always close to NoName, and each time cruel words were spoken, the nasty dragons tightened chains around the boy, crippling and bruising him; and the dragons smeared his eyes with blinding mucous.

As Seeker and his friends continued to watch, they realized that they could hear the cry that was within the boy's heart. On the outside, he was a mean bully, but inside, he was wounded and covered with chains. On the outside he was mumbling curses, but inside he was singing a very sad song...

> *My name is NoName;*
> *And no one cares for me;*
> *But sometime, somewhere*
> *I just know that I will be—*
> *Someone, 'cause somehow, somebody*
> *Is gonna come and be...my friend.*

And then, while NoName sang his song, Seeker and his friends watched in amazement as the King walked right across the Hill toward the boy! Anger and Abuse screamed at the sight of the King and scrambled to get away, rocks flying everywhere.

NoName rubbed his eyes and squinted, like he was trying to see something; and then he went very still and quiet, listening to a song that seemed to pour right into his heart. It was the voice of the King...

> *Your name will be changed—*
> *I speak hope into your life*
> *I'll be your protector*
> *Against the hurt and all the lies*
> *I'll heal what was broken, I'll open your eyes*
> *And I will send a friend to you...*
> *I will be a friend to you...*
> *I...will send a friend...to you*

As NoName listened to the song, he sank down on the hill and wiped tears away from his cheeks. And then, as quickly as he had left, the King was back in the Secret Place, "Wow, King!" KnowSo said, "It was like that kid could really hear you, even though he couldn't see you! That was amazing!"

The children looked back through the Window at NoName. The dragons and their chains vanished, and there was the young boy again, kicking the ground, and acting mean and tough. But now the children understood that he wasn't really mean and tough; he was just very hurt and very lonely.

Seeker's eyes were glistening and his face was flushed, "King!" he cried with excitement, "I'll be his friend! I'll be his friend! Send *me* to be his friend!"

The King turned to Seeker and smiled one of his mysterious smiles. "All right, Seeker; I will send you. But remember, he doesn't believe in me, so he is unable to see my Kingdom; he will not understand what you tell him about me. You must be patient, and keep on being his friend. The dragons have blinded his eyes, but you must *never* fear or worry about any dragons!" The King reached out and firmly placed his hands on the boy's head and continued, "Seeker, I give you *power* over the dragons! I give you *power* to bring NoName...to me!"

Seeker instantly felt much bigger and stronger than he had ever felt before. "Yes, sir!" he said, saluting.

"What can *we do*, King?" Doodle asked excitedly.

"You can wear your armor!" The King smiled another mysterious smile and picked up a copy of the Great Book from where the children had been sitting. (The King had previously given Seeker and his friends their own copy of the Great Book and they always brought it along to read in the Secret Place.) The King opened the Book to the page he wanted and smiled again, "Ah, yes, here it is: The Armor of Light!" As soon as the King spoke, the children saw a cabinet in the corner of the Secret Place that they had never noticed before. The King opened the door of the cabinet and pulled out pieces of shining armor. Seeker and his friends' eyes grew wide. "Wow," they breathed.

"This," declared the King, "is the Armor of Light. You must wear it at all times. It will keep you safe from the dragons, and it will make you strong soldiers in my army!"

"We're in the army again, King?" they asked. (They were remembering an earlier time when the children of the Kingdom had marched forth as soldiers and defeated the dragon Greed by giving and sharing.)

The King laughed. "You've never left my army! You are just learning more about what it really means to be soldiers! Now, let's get you dressed for battle!"

"This is a breastplate—to protect your heart and to help you do what is right. With it, wear this belt called Truth. And here are army shoes. Put them on and always be ready to run and tell people the good news of my Kingdom! Wear this helmet to protect your minds. Remember that you belong to me and nothing can harm you!"

As the King helped them put on the Armor of Light, two

things amazed Seeker and his friends. First of all, they realized that the armor fit them perfectly; and secondly, once the armor was on, they couldn't see it anymore!

The King noticed their expressions and laughed. "You wear my armor by *believing* in it. Every day I want you to take each piece and put it on, knowing that although you can't see it, it is *really* there! And, also know this—even though you can't see it, the dragons can!"

Seeker stood tall, his eyes shining. "Maybe I can't see the Armor of Light, King, but I can feel it!"

The King smiled and said, "This is your shield. It is called Faith. Use it to fight off the lies of the dragons. Believe that I am the King, and I am with you!"

Then the King handed a sparkling sword to each child, which like the other pieces of armor, disappeared from sight as they took hold of it. "Your Sword is the Great Book," explained the King. "As you speak my words, those words will pierce the enemy."

The King put his hands on Dawdle and Slow's hearts, where the shining breastplates fit closely around their chests. "Words have great power. They can hurt...or they can heal. They can bring chains of anger and abuse, or they can set people free. Wear your armor every day. It will help you keep cruel words from penetrating your hearts. As you speak *my* words and refuse to listen to words that hurt, you will be strong soldiers in my army..."

Dawdle and Slow's eyes sparkled as even more of the pain in their hearts was washed away. "Th-Thanks, King!"

"You are all strong soldiers!" the King declared in his most kingly voice. "Seeker will go out and rescue NoName from the dragons. The rest of you must stand guard here in the Secret Place. Stay alert, and watch over him carefully. The Secret Place is where many great battles are fought...and won...for my Kingdom. Study the words of the Great Book. Watch through the Window every day and I will show you the way things really are—not the way they appear to be."

"Yes, Sir!" the children said as they saluted.

The King again put his hands on Seeker and smiled, "According to the words of my Great Book: 'The Spirit of the King is upon you! I have given you power to tell the good news; to heal the brokenhearted; to set prisoners free; and make blind eyes see!' Now, go!"

Seeker bowed before the King, then stood at attention and saluted again, "Yes, sir!"

Chapter Four

Seeker ran out from the Secret Place, down the tower steps, and through the Castle Gardens. He was so filled with a sense of adventure that he was completely surprised when his sister called to him, "Hey! Where are you going in such a hurry?"

"Moira!" Seeker cried, screeching to a halt. "What are you doing here?"

"Spending time in my Secret Place," Moira explained. "It's right over there—the bench under that tree. I've just been talking to the King about my friend, Loneliness. So, where are you going?"

"I'm going on an adventure! I'm going to meet NoName! And look at my Armor of Light!" Seeker pointed proudly to his breastplate.

Moira was puzzled. "NoName? Who's that? And what is the Armor of Light? I don't see any armor!"

"Maybe you can't see it, but it's there! Listen, Moira, I'm in a real hurry! You can find out about the Armor of Light in the King's Great Book. See you later!" And with that, Seeker raced toward the hill that was not too far from the Kingdom.

The path up the Decision Hill was quite steep and hard to climb. Seeker had to pause several times to catch his breath. It took him longer than he expected, and when he finally neared the top, he was relieved to see that NoName was still there—kicking at rocks and looking "tough."

Seeker ran toward him, panting. "Hi!" he called excitedly.

But to Seeker's amazement, NoName was not happy to see him. He turned toward Seeker with a rude glare and shouted, "Stay away from me, kid! Take off!"

Seeker stopped running. He waited a few more minutes to catch his breath, then approached the boy more cautiously. "Uh...hello there...uh...my name is Seeker. What's yours?"

"I said, 'take off'!"

"Take Off? Hmm...that's a nice name; maybe I'll call you T.O. for short!" Seeker laughed at his clever joke, but then noticed that he was the only one laughing.

NoName turned on him and spoke angrily. "Get that stupid grin off your face! Boy, are you ugly! Get away from here, you shrimpy kid!"

For a moment, Seeker didn't know what to do. *I'm sure glad I have the Armor of Light,* he thought to himself. *Words like that used to hurt me, but not anymore! King, please help me...* Then Seeker got an idea. He cleared his throat and said in a friendly voice, "So...do you like rocks?"

"Do I like rocks!?" NoName echoed in disgust. "What do you mean—'Do I like rocks!' What kind of dumb question is that?"

"Well, I just noticed you up here on the hill kicking the rocks. I know how to skip rocks—you know, make them dance across the water. The King taught me."

"Don't give me that stuff about a King!" NoName sneered. "There's no such thing as a King!"

"Oh, yes there is!" Seeker replied. "And he did teach me how to skip rocks...and I'm going to teach you too!"

To NoName's great surprise, Seeker grabbed NoName's hat and raced down the hill. "Hey!" NoName yelled, "Give that back!" Seeker ran as fast as he could down the steep slope. At the bottom of the hill, near the bridge to the Kingdom, was the stream where Seeker spent many hours with the King.

Seeker searched the shore and quickly found some nice, round, smooth stones and showed them to NoName, who angrily grabbed the hat that Seeker tossed to him with a smile. "See? You have to use these kinds of rocks—they remind me of little pancakes!"

"Pancake rocks," NoName sneered. "Who cares?"

Seeker went over to the stream and bent down. He made sure his arm was at the right angle, then tossed the first stone. It danced happily across the top of the water for a short distance, then sank.

Seeker turned to NoName and handed him a stone. "Here! Give it a try!"

NoName shrugged and grabbed the stone, "You're not going to leave me alone until I do, right? Oh, all right, why not dance a pancake rock?" He bent down and threw the stone. It immediately sank. NoName turned away in anger, "See? I knew I couldn't do it! Who cares anyway!"

Seeker reached out and took NoName's arm to stop him from leaving. "Don't give up so fast!" Seeker said. "Let me show you!"

Seeker picked up another stone. "Look," he said. "Keep your arm parallel to the water, and when you toss the stone, flick your wrist...like this..." NoName rolled his eyes and sighed a deep sigh as if trying to tell Seeker how boring this was. Then he took the stone Seeker offered, sighed another bored sigh, and sent the stone skimming over the water. Skip...skip...skip..."You did it!" Seeker cried. "It skipped three times! That was great!"

NoName shrugged and tried to act uninterested as he reached down to pick up another stone. "So...uh...is this one flat enough?" NoName caught on quickly after that, and because he was so strong, one of his stones went skimming across the surface of the water all the way to the other shore!

Seeker was very impressed. "Wow! That rock got all the way over to the Kingdom!" He paused thoughtfully, then said, "It's a great place, you know, the Kingdom.... That's where the King..."

NoName interrupted quickly. "Yeah, right," he said. "Listen kid—no fake stories, OK? Don't give me any of that Kingdom stuff—it's all a bunch of lies." NoName bent to pick up two stones and handed one to Seeker. "Are you up to a challenge?"

Seeker laughed as he and NoName sent the rocks flying across the water. They skipped rocks for a while longer, and then NoName turned to leave. "I have to go now," he said. He walked a short distance, then turned back toward Seeker and looked at him for a long moment. He seemed uncomfortable. Seeker just waited patiently until NoName finally spoke. "Uh...would you...I mean...do you uh...want to skip rocks again tomorrow? You don't have to if you don't want to, I just..."

Seeker interrupted him and said, "Sure! I'll meet you on the hill!" NoName nodded and walked away.

Seeker waited until NoName was out of sight, then put both thumbs up happily, "Thanks, King! And thanks to all my friends for watching out for me from the Secret Place!"

And that was the beginning of a great friendship. Every day Seeker would go to the Secret Place to talk to the King and put on his armor; and every day he would meet NoName on the hill. The two boys built tree houses and forts and explored the forests near the Kingdom. Sometimes, they skipped rocks at the stream or went fishing.

Weeks and months passed. Gradually, the dark and cloudy expression on NoName's face was replaced by a soft sort of friendliness.

"No sign of the dragons anywhere!" Seeker happily reported to his friends one day in the Secret Place. "I think Anger and Abuse have really lost their grip on NoName!"

But Seeker's friends shook their heads. "No, Seeker," warned KnowSo. "Those dragons are still close by. Make sure you wear your armor."

Doodle nodded, "And tell NoName about the King, Seeker! Don't give up. The truth about the King will set him free from the dragons."

Do pointed to the Great Book. "Look, that's what it says right here! 'The truth will set them free.' *Do* it, Seeker! Tell NoName the truth. Don't give up!"

That was good advice, because lately, Seeker *had* given up trying to talk to NoName about the King. Every time Seeker had brought up the subject, NoName refused to listen. "I don't believe in all that stuff," he would say and then mutter angrily under his breath about "fake Kingdom stories."

The next day, after Doodle and Do's encouragement, Seeker had an idea. He and NoName were carrying their fishing poles over their shoulders and walking barefoot across a log to their favorite fishing spot. As they walked, Seeker thought to himself, *He won't let me talk about the King, but he never told me not to sing about the King! It's worth a try...*

When the boys had settled on the bank of the stream and sank their hooks in the water, Seeker leaned back against a tree and casually began to sing one of the King's songs...

> *There is a King who loves you.*
> *There is a King who cares...*

NoName reacted immediately, "Stop it, Seeker! I don't like that kind of music!" Seeker pretended to be hurt, and NoName added quickly, "Besides, you're scaring the fish away!"

"OK, OK!" Seeker said defensively. "I'll just hum it! Maybe the fish will like that!"

Seeker quietly hummed the tune over and over. He glanced over at NoName from time to time with a smile. NoName shook his head at his friend, but Seeker was sure that he saw NoName smiling, too.

Chapter Five

Time passed in the Kingdom of Joy and Peace. As the children continued to meet together in their Secret Place, Seeker's sister, Moira, also spent time in her Secret Place in the Castle Gardens. The King had given her a copy of the Great Book, and the words seemed like they were alive. Every day Moira read and read and read. She, too, had discovered the Armor of Light and had learned to put it on each day. Moira was happier than she had ever been, but her happiness was always shadowed by the sorrow she felt for Loneliness.

One day, in her Secret Place, Moira was talking to the King about her friend again. "Well. King, here I am again. It's been a long time, but I'll just keep asking you about Loneliness. Please, please, please help her to find the way into your Kingdom. She needs you so much. Please help her...and help her little boy. Rescue them from the Darkness. Help them to know the truth about you and to get rid of the lies the dragons have told them..."

Just then, Moira heard someone crying. To her surprise, Slow was walking toward her on the path. "Why, Slow," she said as she went over to the young girl, "what's wrong?"

But Slow couldn't answer. She just cried harder. Moira gave her a tissue and helped her sit down on the bench. After quite a long time, Slow finally said, "W-W-Words."

"Words?" Moira echoed.

Slow nodded. "W-W-Words really hurt. I-I wish that Dawdle and I could talk b-b-better and w-w-walk better. Then people wouldn't s-s-say such mean things to us."

Moira shook her head, "No, Slow. Cruel words can be spoken to you even if you talk and walk the same as other people. It's what you *do* when the words are spoken—that's what matters. Have you been wearing your armor?"

Slow nodded, then shook her head, "S-S-Sometimes I forget. And sometimes...well, sometimes, I just feel t-t-too young to be a soldier."

"Sometimes...like today?" Moira asked gently.

Slow nodded and smiled as she blew her nose again. "B-B-But I know that's not right. Little s-s-soldiers can be very powerful in the K-K-King's army." Then after a long sigh, Slow continued, "I feel better. Thanks, Moira. I think I'm r-r-ready to go back to the S-S-Secret Place and get my armor! I didn't put it on yet t-t-today."

"You can put it on right here!" Moira smiled. "The Secret Place is wherever you meet with the King. All you have to do is call his name, and he will be with you—although you might not see him!" Moira opened the Great Book and pointed, "Here is where it explains about the Armor of Light. You take each piece and put it on; even though you can't see it; it is really there! Look...a helmet, a sword...even boots for those soldiers who happen to have little feet!"

Slow laughed and was marching around the King's Gardens when Dawdle suddenly burst through one of the shrubs. He spoke more quickly than he had ever spoken before, "Hu-Hurry, Slow!" he panted. "Emer-mergency meeting in the S-S-Secret Place! S-S-Seeker is in trouble!"

Chapter Six

Earlier that day Seeker had made the same mistake Slow had made: he hadn't put on his armor.

Things are going so great with NoName, he had thought to himself. *Those dragons are miles away from here now! And pretty soon, NoName is going to start believing the truth, and everything's going to be just fine!* So, instead of taking time in the Secret Place, Seeker just whistled happily on his way across the Kingdom bridge to meet NoName.

When Seeker arrived at the Hill, NoName was sitting in the grass, waiting for him. "Seeker, sit down for a minute," NoName said, patting the ground beside him. "I've been thinking about you, Seeker. I've been thinking about you a lot. And I've been wondering...well...uh...what are you seeking for?"

"What am I seeking for?" Seeker echoed thoughtfully as he sat down. "Hmm, I guess I just want to know more about the King...Yeah, I'm seeking to know more about the King."

"But, you don't *really* believe in that stuff about a King, do you?" asked NoName.

"Of course I do!" replied Seeker, "I *really* believe in it! It's the truth!"

NoName looked at his friend, then continued, "The truth, huh? So, tell me, *if* there *is* a King, where does he live?"

"What do you mean, where does he live? He lives right over there in the Castle!" Seeker stood and pointed. His heart began to beat faster as he realized what was happening. *This is so great! I just knew he was close to believing the truth!*

NoName stood up and peered intently in the direction Seeker pointed. "What Castle? I just see trees!"

"Oh yeah, you can't see it yet," said Seeker, remembering that NoName's eyes had been blinded by the dragons. "Well, there really is a Castle, NoName, and there really is a King! And he *really* loves you!"

NoName peered harder and said earnestly, "He does?"

Suddenly, it was as though Seeker was looking through the Window of the Secret Place. He saw NoName the same way he had seen him that first day—crippled, bruised, and wounded, with chains wrapped all around him. But now, the chains were much looser than they had been, and his eyes weren't covered with the oozing, slimy screen—they were starting to open!

Seeker was so happy that he laughed and hugged NoName. "Your eyes are starting to open! This is so great! You're starting to understand!"

"I am?" NoName asked. "Yeah...I guess I am!"

NoName rubbed his eyes and looked again toward the Kingdom, "Hey...I think I can see a Castle! Yes, I *do* see the Castle! Wow! It's so white it sparkles! This is awesome!"

"Yes!" Seeker cried happily, "Very, very awesome!"

But suddenly, the air became cool, the sky darkened, and as if appearing from nowhere, Anger and Abuse came raging up the hill toward the two boys. And it was then that Seeker realized he didn't have on the Armor of Light.

The fiery green breath of Anger and Abuse smelled as though they had never, ever brushed their teeth, and their breath burned Seeker's heart as they snarled past him toward NoName. The dragons held their claws over the boy's eyes, blinding him once again with their oozing mucous. They tightened the chains with a determined pull, and then, with terrifying fierceness, the dragons roared at Seeker.

NoName stood on the hill, angry and confused. He looked at Seeker, then stepped back, shook his head, and cried, "Lies! Lies! Listen Seeker, don't you ever talk to me about the King again! I don't believe it! It's not the truth! I don't believe it! Get away from me! Never come near me again with your stupid, fake Kingdom stories! Get away from me!"

With that, NoName lifted his hand to hit Seeker. Seeker dodged just in time. Fear rose up within Seeker's heart. NoName's face was dark with an evil sort of cloudiness. *The dragons,* Seeker thought in horror, *The dragons have control of him! And here I am without my armor!* Seeker dodged another swoop of NoName's fists.

"NoName!" he cried. "It's me, Seeker! Please, just listen to me!" Seeker dodged yet another blow. "NoName, please! I'm your friend, remember?"

It was at that moment that Moira, Dawdle, and Slow reached the Secret Place. "Hurry!" HopeSo cried. "Seeker is trying to fight the battle alone."

The children gathered at the window and peered through the Darkness to see Seeker dodging NoName's fists.

"He forgot to wear his armor," Do said.

"And he forgot to take his sword," Doodle added, holding up Seeker's copy of the Great Book that was lying in the Secret Place. "He's trying to use his own words, but his own words aren't powerful enough."

Moira nodded. "He needs to use the *King's* words."

"Yes!" Yes cried. "He needs to use his sword!"

"C-C-Can we take it to him?" Dawdle wondered. "Or d-d-does he need to come h-h-here to the Secret Place to get it?"

Slow shot a smile toward Moira, "He c-can have a Secret Place right where he is. He just n-needs to call out to the King!"

Moira smiled back and then said, "Listen everyone, the Great Book says there is power when two or more ask something in the Secret Place together. Let's ask, together, for Seeker to call on the King."

"OK, Moira," the children nodded.

"We'll *do* it!" announced Doodle.

The children joined hands with Moira, and with one voice, they shouted through the Window of the Secret Place, "Call upon the King! Seeker, call upon the King!"

By now, NoName had dropped down on the ground. He was pounding his fists into the grass, and crying, but he refused to let Seeker come near. Anger and Abuse were picking their noses, sneering wickedly, and pulling the chains tighter around the young boy. *I don't know what to do,* Seeker thought. *I can't just leave him here! And it's gotten so dark! I don't know if I could even find my way back to the Kingdom bridge! I need help. I need...the King! Of course! What have I been thinking?* Seeker closed his eyes tightly and whispered, "King! King, please help me! I'm so sorry for not putting on my armor..."

"Then put it on now!" said a familiar voice.

Seeker wheeled around in surprise. There, in the middle of the Darkness, stood the King. "King! You're here!" Seeker cried, hugging the King in relief. "But how can I put on my armor? I left it in the Secret Place!"

The King smiled. "The Secret Place is wherever you meet with me, Seeker. Now go ahead, put your armor on! The King handed each piece of armor to Seeker, and then leaned forward, winked, and disappeared from his sight. As Seeker put on his armor, he immediately felt stronger. He stood tall, and his eyes were shining as he turned back toward NoName...and Anger and Abuse.

The dragons had been watching.

They had watched the King appear...then disappear. They had watched Seeker put on the Armor of Light. And as the dragons watched, they had become very, very afraid. "Uh-oh," they said anxiously, their bad breath coming in nervous gasps. They still had firm grips on the chains around NoName, but their claws were shaking so badly that they couldn't pick their noses.

When Seeker turned toward them, Anger and Abuse tried their best to look fierce and unafraid. They roared loudly and tightened the chains around NoName, who cried out with pain so deep that suddenly, Seeker became absolutely furious. "Leave him alone! Do you hear me, dragons?" he shouted. "NoName was just starting to see—just starting to understand! His eyes were just beginning to open!" Seeker stomped his foot and cried, "I've had it with you dragons!"

The dragons belched rudely. "And we've had it with you, too!" they mocked. "The kid stays with us!" Anger and Abuse pulled the chains more tightly around NoName.

Then Seeker heard the King's voice speaking to him. "Don't hold a conversation with them, Seeker," the King said. "I have given you power to bring NoName into my Kingdom. You have *power* over those dragons! Go ahead, Seeker!"

Seeker felt strength from the King's words. "Oh yeah! Power! The King has given me power!" Seeker rolled up his shirtsleeves, adjusted the Armor of Light (which he couldn't see but knew was there), clenched his fists, and called out with confident authority, "*Dragons!*"

The dragons looked around anxiously, desperately trying to pick their noses while hanging on to NoName.

"*Dragons!*" Seeker repeated, "I order you to get your claws off that kid right now!"

Seeker's words came with such force that the dragons yelled out in pain, but they continued their hold on NoName.

Seeker's heart filled with determination. He rolled his sleeves up a bit farther, took a deep breath, and said in a low, meaningful voice, "Now you listen here, dragons! The King has given me *power* over you! I said get your claws off that kid right now!" The dragons cried out again with pain, but still held tightly to NoName.

The King spoke quietly. "Use your sword, Seeker."

Without seeing it, but knowing it was there, Seeker held out his sword. With great authority in his voice, he declared words from the Great Book. "The Spirit of the King is upon me! He has given me power to tell his good news; to heal the brokenhearted; to set prisoners free and make blind eyes see! In the Name of the King, you dragons—*go!*"

Although he didn't realize it, Seeker's friends and his sister, Moira, were speaking the same words from the Great Book. And as they spoke, they saw a Light more brilliant than any light. The Light cut right through the Darkness and wrapped itself protectively around NoName. "The people who walked in Darkness have seen a great Light!" Moira cried. "Those who walked in the dragon's land—upon them the Light has shined!"

Meanwhile, the dragons frantically held their ears and cried out in pain. The words from the Great Book pierced and cut their grip on the chains surrounding NoName. The Light pushed them backward, and with each powerful word from the Great Book, Anger and Abuse grew smaller and smaller and smaller. They moaned in agony until, with one final whimper of defeat, the dragons slithered away, all the way back to their master in the deep, dark place beneath the trap door of Selfishness.

Seeker watched and then realized how very tired he felt. With a deep sigh, he leaned on his sword and sank down onto his knees. After a few moments, Seeker looked across the hill toward NoName. What he saw brought a flood of tears to his eyes.

Light covered the hillside. Huge, amazing, warm, overpowering, wonderful, golden light! NoName was rubbing his eyes and laughing and crying all at the same time. His eyes were finally open, and he was looking at the one who had broken the dragons' power, the one who lived in the Light...the one who really, really loved him....

And in the next instant, NoName ran into the arms of the King.

Chapter Seven

"**N**oName and the King!" Seeker whispered. "NoName and the King! Hey, why am I whispering? I should be yelling with everything I've got to yell with!" Seeker began jumping up and down and shouting, "NoName and the King! Hey, dragons! Hey, everybody in the Secret Place—look! Hey, everybody in the whole world! NoName and the King! They're finally together! Hooray! Hooray! NoName and the King!"

Seeker started doing cartwheels across Decision Hill. In the Secret Place, all of his friends were jumping up and down and yelling, too. Then Moira said, "Shhh!" and called them all to look again through the Window of the Secret Place. Seeker turned at the same time and realized that the King was singing.

The King was singing the most beautiful song that NoName had ever heard. The words of the song were words from the Great Book—powerful words that brought healing and strength to every place where, throughout NoName's life, other words had torn and bruised and crippled him.

As the King sang, he removed the chains. He healed what had been bruised and broken. And NoName was brought out of Darkness into the Kingdom of Light.

I was once wounded...like you.
I was once wounded for you;
I felt your pain;
I took your pain.

I am acquainted with sorrow.
I was despised and rejected;

I was hurt, and afflicted;
I took your grief,
So that you might have peace;
I bore your sins and transgressions.

Now you are healed—I am your healer.
You are healed—I make you whole.
See the chains fall aside;
I have opened your eyes;
And I, I am your healer.

The King helped the boy to his feet, and put an arm around his shoulders. Then the King looked over at Seeker and waved for him to come. Seeker hurried across the Hill. While the King smiled one of his mysterious smiles, the two friends hugged, laughed, and cried together.

"This is so great!" Seeker said. "This is just so great!"

"Seeker," said the King, "This—is 'NewName'!"

"NewName?" echoed Seeker. "Wow! Welcome to the Kingdom! This is just so great!"

The boys hugged again. "Thanks for being my friend, Seeker," NewName said. "Thanks for telling me about the King. And thanks for not giving up."

Seeker gave his friend a handclap, then looked closely at his eyes. "Can you see the Castle now? No more trees? Can you see the Castle?"

"I can see it, Seeker. I really can!"

"OK. Look harder. There's one especially tall tower—it's my Secret Place!"

"Secret Place?" NewName squinted and strained to see. "I think I see an especially tall tower...but all the towers look pretty special to me!"

"Well anyway, my friends and I have been meeting there and

doing battles against the dragons this whole time! And we've learned all about the Armor of Light and..."

"Dragons?" NewName echoed. "What dragons? Armor of Light? What's that?"

"You'll find out, NewName!" Seeker said happily. "Wow, King, what an adventure this has been!"

"And it's not over yet, Seeker," the King said as he put his great arms around both boys and smiled a most mysterious smile. "NewName needs a place to live for a while. Do you happen to know where he could stay?"

"What?" Seeker asked, confused. "No, I don't think so...but I'm sure we could find someplace."

The King smiled again, "Hmm...Well, I thought you might just know of a nice, cozy little room that's just waiting for someone like NewName to move into."

"Nice, cozy little room?" Seeker echoed. His mind went blank for a moment. Then Seeker looked up at the King with wide-open eyes. The attic room! Of course! "Yeah, King! Yeah, I sure do know a nice, cozy little room! My mom changed the attic room into a bedroom...just like you told her to, King! You had it planned out all along, didn't you? Wow! This is all so great. NewName can stay at our place!" He turned to NewName excitedly, "You can stay with us!"

The King nodded. "That's good, Seeker, because your sister, Moira, has been spending time with me in her Secret Place... talking to me about NewName's mother...."

At this, Moira leaned farther through the Window to hear the King speak. "NewName's mother?" she echoed out loud. "But I don't know NewName's mother! What does the King mean?"

The King looked through the Window of the Secret Place at Moira, winked, and continued speaking, "Moira has been talking to me about NewName's mother. Her name is Loneliness. And I am going to meet her...right now."

Think About the Story

Do you know anyone like NoName? Do you know someone who looks and acts tough on the outside? It is probably because they are hurting on the inside. It is probably because they need a friend. Go to the Secret Place! Let the King show you how to pray; let Him give you the power and the spiritual tools you need to bring people out of the Darkness, to Him. Or perhaps you yourself are like NoName. Perhaps you have been full of anger and abuse, pain, and hurt on the inside. King Jesus can heal you.

Talk to the King

"King Jesus, You see the real, inside me. People see the outside; but You see my heart. You know the anger, the bitterness, the pain, and the loneliness that I feel sometimes. Today, I ask You to help me. Please help me to forgive people who have said or done things to me that were mean or wrong. Help me to wear Your Armor of Light every day. And please help me to bring Your healing to the hurting people around me. I want my life to truly be an adventure! Help me to be a seeker!"

Read from the King's Great Book—Luke 4:18

The King came to heal the brokenhearted and to set the prisoners free!

He opens up the eyes that were blinded.
Look at Luke chapter 4:18
(Great Book Paraphrase)

- **Matthew 6:6—Go into the Secret Place**

- **Jeremiah 33:3—Let the King show you things**

- **Romans 13:12—The "Armor of Light"**

- **Ephesians 6:11-17—The pieces of armor**

- **Isaiah 53:3-5—The King suffered... for you**

Part Seven

Carriers of the Kingdom

Carriers of the Kingdom—The Song

I am a carrier of the Kingdom
Because the King lives in me.
I'm a carrier of the Kingdom
But my load's not heavy...
Carrier of the Kingdom
That's what I'm called to be...
I want the light...of eternal life
To shine bright through me.
Because when the light shines
in the middle of darkness
People who've wandered will find the way—
And the Great Book says, the Kingdom is in us
It says we're a temple, a castle, a dwelling place
For the King of all kings!

Introduction

NewName raced up the Straight and Narrow Path, tripped over his shoelace, and tumbled into a bush near the Doorkeeper. "Ooops!" he cried, dusting leaves off his shirt. "Am I late? Is Seeker here yet? What about the other kids?"

The Doorkeeper smiled, "No, you aren't late, NewName. In fact, you are right on time! The King is waiting for you."

"Great! Then I'll just sit with you until everyone else gets here!" NewName settled down on the grass beside the castle door and continued talking, hardly taking a breath, "Mr. Doorkeeper, did you know that my mom and I just moved into a house on the same street as Seeker and his family? I *really* like living in Peace and Harmony! And did you know that my mom used to be Loneliness and the King changed her name to Compassion? And did you..."

"Excuse me, NewName," the Doorkeeper interrupted with another smile, "but did *you* know that the King is waiting for you?"

"What!" NewName stood up, startled. "He's waiting for *me?* I thought you meant he was waiting for all of us!"

The Doorkeeper opened the castle door, bowing and motioning for NewName to enter. "The others will be here soon, but right now, the King wants to see *you*. Come, I will take you to his throne room."

NewName's heart thumped hard in his chest while he walked with the Doorkeeper down the long shining hallway. The young boy had been reading the King's Great Book and learning as much as he could about life in the Kingdom. He had spent many hours with the King over the past few months, but never by himself; Seeker and the other children were always there, too. "Wow!" NewName whispered to himself, "All by myself to see the King. What am I going to say? What is *he* going to say? What are *we* going to say?"

The Doorkeeper stopped at the entrance to the Grand Throne Room, bowed, and motioned for NewName to continue on his own. NewName's knees were trembling as he walked across the great golden room, knelt before the throne, and looked up at the King.

"Hi." The word came out of NewName's mouth with a little squeak. He felt embarrassed but the King smiled and responded in his deep, rich voice, "Hi."

There was a brief silence, then NewName said, "I really like living in your Kingdom."

"I *know*," the King said, still smiling. He patted the chair next to his throne. "Come sit beside me. I want to show you something."

NewName gasped and then hurried to sit beside the King. The chair was covered with thick velvet and the arms were made of solid gold. "Wow," he breathed, "I feel like a prince."

"Good!" the King replied, "because that is who you are!" The King noticed NewName's expression and continued, "You moved from Darkness to my Kingdom of Light. Every person who gives their life to me is adopted into my family, and that makes them royalty! Now, Prince NewName, look at this..."

The King unrolled a parchment map, and NewName studied it for a moment, then pointed. "There's your castle! And there's the Bridge...and there's...'Decision Hill.' Is that hill where Seeker met me, King? I'm sure glad you sent him to be my friend; I'm sure glad he told me about you."

"Me, too," the King nodded, "And there are many other people who need to hear about me and my Kingdom. Will you tell them?" As NewName nodded earnestly, the King pointed again to the map, "Today you will go on an adventure! And this is where I will send you and the other children: The 'Land of Laws Forgotten.' You will help the people to remember."

"What have they forgotten, King?"

"They have forgotten the truth about me," the King answered, "There are some who knew the truth, but decided to go their own way, and others who *really* don't want to hear anything about my Kingdom. And now the children in that land have names like Clutter, Chaos, and Confusion, Hostility and Trouble, Scoffer and Slander."

"They need new names!" NewName declared.

The King nodded. "Yes, they do! And I thought that *you* might like to help me give them their new names."

"Me?" NewName was shocked. "You want *me* to help you?"

"Yes, I do!" the King said with a laugh. "Now c'mon! Seeker and the others have reached the Secret Place. I asked them to meet us there. It is time for all of you to see the children of Laws Forgotten...through the Window of the Secret Place."

With a twinkle in his eyes, the King bent close to NewName and winked. "Would you like to race?"

And with that, the King was off! NewName was laughing so much it was hard to keep up as the King slid down one shining hallway after another, then ran up the winding tower stairway to the Secret Place.

Chapter One

When NewName and the King reached the Secret Place, Seeker, Giggles, HopeSo, KnowSo, Doodle, and Do were waiting. "Where are the others?" NewName asked. Just as the King began to explain how he had sent the other Kingdom children on a different kind of adventure, the door gently swung open and a very beautiful woman entered the Secret Place. "Mom!" NewName cried, running to give her a big hug. "This is great! I didn't know you would be here!"

"Welcome, Compassion," the King said, calling NewName's mother to stand beside him, and then he turned to the children. "From now on, I want you to bring Compassion with you whenever you are in the Secret Place. There is much you can learn from her."

"Hi," said Compassion, her voice rich and warm and beautiful. Seeker and his friends immediately felt right at home with NewName's mother; it was like she *really* belonged with them in the Secret Place, but Doodle and Do were scratching their heads, wondering. "Compassion is sure a big word," said Doodle, "*Do* you know what it means, KnowSo?"

All the children looked at KnowSo expectantly; he always seemed to know things, and sure enough, he nodded, "It means *really* caring."

The King was smiling. "Yes, *really* caring. As I said, there is much you can learn from her; Compassion will help you to see people the way I want you to see them...like the people I want you to see today," the King said as he opened the Window, "The people who live in the Land of Laws Forgotten."

The children gathered closely and peered through the Window, and NewName explained, "The King wants us to help the people in Laws Forgotten to *remember* his laws, and there are some kids there who *really* need new names!"

Through the Window of the Secret Place the children saw the lands beyond the Kingdom. Quickly their eyes skimmed over the CARNALville of Selfishness, where they used to spend their time, before they *really* knew the King. Then, Seeker and his friends spent a moment checking on the Village of Generosity.

"The people in Generosity sure look happy!" said Seeker. The others agreed.

"Look!" Giggles pointed, "There's Moira and Daring, Dawdle and Slow, and Gladness and Glee, and Yes!"

"They are on their way to visit Generosity," the King explained. "The people there are still learning about loving to give and..."

"Not loving to get!" the children said together.

"DO you remember the nasty dragon that used to rule them?" asked Doodle.

"Yes I DO!" Do nodded.

"The dragon Greed," said KnowSo. "Will he stay away forever, King?"

The King shook his head. "Greed will always try to regain control, but for now he's spending most of his time somewhere else...a place where he feels....welcome."

"Look!" HopeSo pointed, "There's Royal Harbor! Remember when we sailed on Daring's ship and rescued Wanderer, I mean Steadfast, from the Island of Despair?"

"How's your dad *doing* these days, Seeker?" Doodle asked.

"Pretty good," Seeker responded. "I see him really often, and we spend time doing things like skipping rocks at the stream. He's living in one of the guest rooms at Castle Rock because he's still not ready to come home yet, right, King?"

The King nodded. "Learning to overcome obstacles with opposites takes some people a long time."

They looked again through the Window, glancing briefly at the Valley of Lost Dreams where the King had rescued Seeker's sister, Moira, and where Compassion had lived when her name was Loneliness. Then, as the children watched, their eyes opened to see another dark and dismal country and the King pointed, "The Land of Laws Forgotten."

"The Land of Laws Forgotten," Seeker echoed, peering through the darkness, "It definitely sounds like the people who live there need to know the King, and there are probably dragons around, too!"

"Dragons," Giggles nodded solemnly, not giggling at all.

Compassion moved closer to them as they peered through the gloomy haze, and this is what Seeker and his friends saw:

The children of Laws Forgotten were in a dark alley, some leaning against crumbling brick walls and some sitting on old boxes and crates. Clutter was searching through his huge bag of possessions. "I know I had them this morning! What did you do with them?" he demanded, while Chaos and Confusion nervously bent to search their own huge bags.

Hostility's face was dark and angry, "It was your job to make sure we had tickets for Empty Entertainment Theatre!" she yelled. "Why do you guys always make simple stuff so complicated? Now what are we going to do all day?"

"Has anyone seen my glasses?" Confusion asked, fumbling through his bag.

"They're on top of your head, like usual," Scoffer sneered, and Slander laughed rudely.

Confusion felt the top of his head, sheepishly put on his glasses, and then pointed, "Hey look...here comes Trouble!"

Hostility sighed in angry relief, "Good old Trouble! He always shows up when there's nothing to do! Hey, Trouble," she called,

"We were supposed to go to Empty Entertainment Theatre today but Clutter, Chaos, and Confusion messed things up, like usual!" The three brothers resumed their frantic search for the tickets, and Hostility asked Trouble, "Do you have any ideas about what we can do today?"

Trouble sauntered over to them with a sly smirk. He was snapping his fingers, humming, and moving his shoulders in time to some inner beat. Trouble always seemed to know a song about going places and doing things that were unusual and a little bit scary. Beside him was a ragged orphan girl they called Little One. Little One was jogging, trying to keep up to her hero's big steps. She had been close to Trouble for a long time, but lately she had felt concerned about him; his songs had become sad and depressing, and sometimes he would get really angry and yell about how his father, and then his mother, had abandoned him. Little One had decided to stay even closer to Trouble and try to help.

Trouble pretended to be surprised by Hostility's question, "Do *I* have any ideas?" he asked, pushing his cap to one side mischievously.

Little One caught on right away and spoke with similar surprise, "Does *he* have any ideas? Trouble *always* has great ideas!" *I just hope his next idea won't be too sad or depressing or scary,* she thought to herself.

"I have an especially great idea for you today!" Trouble said, motioning for the group to come closer and looking around to make sure that no one was watching them.

The children leaned toward Trouble. "What are we going to do, Trouble?"

"Shhh!" Trouble lowered his voice and spoke in a convincing whisper. "It's—the Government Show!"

"Government Show? What's that? Where is it?" the children questioned. Hostility, however, drew back. "Government Show?" she repeated.

"I know!" said Scoffer. "Down at Government Hall! Haven't you ever heard about those guys? It's really something! First it's like one big party, and then all they do is yell at each other!"

"Yeah," nodded Hostility. "Just like home."

The children looked at Hostility and agreed, "Yeah. Just like home."

"The best part is," Trouble continued with his convincing whisper, "that no kids are allowed!"

"No kids are allowed!" the children said with new interest. (There were no rules in Laws Forgotten. The children were allowed to wander wherever they pleased.)

"No kids allowed," Trouble repeated, "Especially...not in the balcony! The Ruling Opposition declared that a long time ago."

"Let's go! This is one cool idea! Trouble, we're with you!"

"And I—am with you!" Trouble laughed and stepped into the lead.

Little One held back, considering Trouble's idea. It seemed harmless enough. It certainly wasn't sad or depressing like some of his ideas lately. She was about to run to catch up with the others when she noticed Hostility still leaning against the wall, frowning. "Wait a minute, everyone!" Little One called, "Hey, Hostility, c'mon!"

Hostility's face was even more dark and angry than usual. "Nah. My folks would really 'get hostile' if they saw me down there." She yanked her sleeves down over her hands, and the others looked at each other, remembering the bruises on Hostility's arms. Hostility always wore long sleeves to cover them. "Just go!" she snapped. "I'll find something else to do; I don't care."

Trouble moved beside Hostility. "Oops! I forgot all about your dad being the Ruling Opposition and that Lady Strife is your mother! Listen, no one, especially your mom and dad, will know that we're there! We'll sneak in and watch from the balcony—nice and quiet..." Trouble looked meaningfully at the others.

The children nodded and held their hands solemnly over their hearts. "Nice and quiet."

Hostility looked from one face to the next. "Promise you'll be good?"

The others immediately put on their most earnest and sincere expressions, and again held their hands over their hearts, "Promise!"

"Oh, all right then," Hostility said gruffly, as she moved to the front to walk with Trouble, and off they went to Government Hall.

Chapter Two

Government Hall was a huge, dark stone building. The door was so heavy that it took three of the children to open it. They were afraid that someone would try to stop them from going inside, but there was so much noisy disorder going on that the children were able to sneak up into the balcony unnoticed. Hostility did get worried, however, when Clutter rummaged around in his pack and pulled out several bags of popcorn, "Here, enjoy the show!" Hostility began munching just as loudly as the rest when she realized that no one, not even her parents, knew they were there.

Hostility's father, the Ruling Opposition, was standing in the center of the room, and beside him was her mother, Strife. The room was decorated like a lavish country club, and the city leaders sat around small ornate tables eating a wide variety of candy-coated foods. Musicians played in the background, and the noise of bantering and discussion filled the room.

"Now that's what I call an opposition party!" Scoffer mocked.

"So, this is how they run our land," Slander snickered, taking out a notebook and writing down what he saw. (Slander always kept track of details just in case he could use them to hurt someone sometime.)

As the noise and music grew louder, the Ruling Opposition banged the floor with his cane, displaying pompous authority and trying to gain control. But actually, Opposition had *never* been in control of Laws Forgotten.

Crouched in the background, ever present but never seen, were some very rude and disgusting, smelly, slobbering, belching, nose-picking...dragons. Their names were Pride, Greed, and Corruption. The dragons had ruled people throughout the World Beyond the Kingdom, and especially those people within the Land of Laws Forgotten, for a long time. In fact, the dragons had controlled Laws Forgotten for as long as the people could *not* remember. Pride, Greed, and Corruption lurked in the shadows of thinking and reasoning and decision-making. They breathed nasty dark thoughts into the minds of the leaders and citizens, causing mistrust and conflict throughout the land.

Today, the dragons stood especially close to Hugh Manism (Director of Schools), M.T. Entertainment (owner of several shops and theatres), and Strife (Hostility's mother and Opposition's wife). Strife poked her husband sharply in the ribs, and hissed, "Start the meeting!"

Opposition banged his cane on the floor with greater pompous authority, "Order! Order!" he shouted. To his pleased surprise, everyone became quiet. He turned to the city leaders on his right, then his left, and then to his wife, "Welcome... welcome...and...most welcome." He nodded to the court minstrel, who in turn blew a call on his trumpet and lead the assembly in song. Everyone was completely unaware that their singing was directed by three very evil dragons, and although they thought they were singing a magnificent song, it was actually a terrible noise. When it came to the verses, each person sang a different tune, with different words, and each one tried to sing louder than the others to make sure their song was heard; but they did manage to at least sing the chorus together....

Laws Forgotten Song

We earnestly endeavor to keep this land forever
The Land of Laws Forgotten!
From higher law we've turned aside

And very person can decide—
to do what's right in their own eyes

The Land of Laws Forgotten!

Verse 1

How can we declare some law
When every person has a cause,
And every clause in each new law's affected?
There's no such thing as right or wrong—
Bring your ideas—every one!
And every single right will be protected!

Verse 2

That's right—we have rights—Because we believe
In the ultimate good of mankind, you see
People are victims; their behavior's excused
Because of whatever excuses they use....
Can't you see—there's absolutely
No such thing as truth—it's really
What you and me define it to be
It's personal philo-o-o-osophy!

Verse 3

It is absolutely true—no such thing as absolute
Truth is relative with who we are speaking—
Relatively speaking.
No more moral implications
Call it situation ethics
And whatever seems to have the best support!
Just be plural and inclusive,
Trying not to be exclusive
Exclusive is the last resort!

Verse 4

It is all a game where we choose
Our ways we—make up new rules
Doing what it is we want to do....
I have the right to say
That you're wrong and you can't play and
All the rights have left—and gone away
I don't want you on my team
Because it's all about ME

The volume of the song grew to such intensity that a woman who had just entered the hall had to stomp her feet and yell to get their attention. "Hello? Hello? Are you going to go on like this all day? Will you just remember why you are here!"

Everyone was amazed at being interrupted. Opposition regained his composure and loudly cleared his throat. "Why we are here...Why we are here..." He turned to Strife with a blank expression. "Why *are* we here, anyway?"

Strife poked him again sharply and he said, "Of course! Of course! We are here today to allow citizens of the Land of Laws Forgotten to bring their issues to our attention. And we have some fine, yes some very fine, citizens here with us to do that very thing. Now then, this worthy citizen is..."

"Mom!" In the balcony, Clutter, Chaos, and Confusion almost choked on their popcorn. "What's she doing here?"

"Shh!" the others warned; and the three boys sat down, bewildered.

Opposition continued, "This worthy citizen is Lady Affluence! She is, as you all know very well, the owner of many of our prestigious downtown businesses."

Affluence moved to the center of the hall, her jewels and rich clothing shimmering, and she was very much aware that everyone in the room watched in admiration. The dragons, Pride and Greed, strolled at her side, purring as she spoke, "Ruling Opposition, I see your lavish, wasteful party, and I assume that our little...*business* arrangement...is working out well for both of us..."

"Business arrangement?" Opposition sputtered, the dragon Corruption at his side. "But I thought that was under-handed... I mean, hand it over...let's table that idea...I mean put it under the table....I mean....I mean I look forward to your backing....I mean...I need your backing to move forward. Oh, can we just meet in the lobby?"

"Yes, you *do* need my backing," Affluence crooned, "if you want to be renamed as the Ruling Opposition of Laws Forgotten, and you will need *all* of our backing, *remember!*"

"Yes, you need our backing, just as we need yours!" shouted M.T. Entertainment. "What about the special signs for my new amusement theatre? You promised them in exchange for support from the Empty Entertainment Industry! You said they would be here last week—and I have a *right* to know where they are!"

"Rights!" someone shouted. "We have rights!"

Hugh Manism pushed forward with narrowed eyes, "Speaking of rights...what about the funding you promised for the purchase of the new school textbook, 'Everyone's Rules are Right?' It will be an asset to the entire educational system, which, I might point out, is positively thriving under my direction!" The dragon Pride moved close, and Hugh Manism pushed his chest forward and boasted, "Under my direction, the children of our great land are self-motivated, self-assertive, self-reliant, and self-assured! They have self-awareness, self-esteem, and self-confidence. As a result, they are increasingly self-helped, self-regulated, and self-affirming! They practice self-talk, self-improvement, and self-importance! They have completely turned away from any higher laws and..."

While Hugh Manism continued boasting, Strife started to argue with M.T. Entertainment, and Opposition and Affluence met in the lobby. The dragons prowled unseen in their midst, breathing proud, greedy, and corrupt thoughts into their minds, all the while growing stronger and more and more powerful.

Clutter, Chaos, Confusion, Scoffer, Slander, and Trouble were leaning on the edge of the balcony. They watched with Hostility until Little One said, "Every single one of those city leaders thinks they are right! Which one is right, anyway? Or is there any such thing as right? Is there any such thing as wrong? And does right or wrong even matter?"

Clutter, Chaos, and Confusion looked at her with blank expressions and shrugged nervously, "We are so confused!"

Scoffer yawned loudly, "Boring!" she declared.

Trouble stood to his feet with a big stretch. "There's no such thing as wrong or right," he said. "It's like those city leaders sang about. Life is just a game. It's a game where there are no rules. No right. No wrong. You live. You die. The end."

Scoffer nodded. "Yeah, life is a game, and the city leaders keep cheating and changing the rules!"

Trouble paced for a few minutes, humming softly and snapping his fingers. The look on his face made Little One feel concerned again. What was going on in his mind? Then Trouble stopped humming and said, "I have an idea."

Little One stiffened, wondering what kind of idea it might be. The children looked at each other and responded sarcastically, "Another one? Is it any better than this one?"

"Well..." said Trouble, "I've just been wondering what's behind that door..."

The children followed his gaze to a small door off in one corner of the balcony. Little One relaxed. It *did* look rather interesting. It looked as though no one had opened it for a long, long time.

Trouble spoke softly, "I've also been wondering what could be so important around here that no kids are allowed. It's sure not the government show!"

The others murmured their agreement. "Let's see where it goes," Little One whispered, excitement in her voice. She went over to the door and cautiously touched the metal handle, then immediately pulled back her hand with a shudder. Cobwebs covered her fingers. "M...maybe this isn't such a good idea," she stammered.

Hostility frowned and looked over the balcony at her parents, and Trouble stepped forward reassuringly. "Don't worry. They'll never notice. Besides, we're just kids. We're supposed to be curious!" He winked and said, "And like those city leaders teach us: there's no such thing as right or wrong, remember?"

And with that, Trouble reached for the handle and tugged on the door.

Chapter Three

As the door opened, dust flew everywhere and the old wooden frame creaked loudly. The children looked anxiously toward the citizens and rulers in Government Hall, but no one noticed; the endless noise continued.

Trouble pulled the door back just enough for them to slip through. It took several moments for their eyes to adjust to the semi-darkness; then they saw a narrow staircase. With their hearts pounding in suspense, the children carefully tiptoed up the creaking stairs. They found themselves in a large attic room. A thick layer of dust covered the collection of desks, tables, filing cabinets, boxes, and piles of books. Clutter, Chaos, and Confusion sneezed in unison, while Trouble opened the shutters of the one and only tiny window to let in some air.

A hush fell over the group as they picked their way through the cobwebs, exploring the piles of books and boxes. The only sound was Trouble's fingers snapping and his low hum. Little One's voice broke the silence. "Wow...look at this...." The others quickly went to a desk where Little One was trying to pull out a huge book from the bottom drawer. Trouble helped her lift it onto the desk and together they blew away a thick layer of dust. "It's called 'The Great Book'..." Little One whispered. Everyone felt a sense of awe as they gathered around the book. It seemed to be very important and very old. With a hesitant look at her friends, who nodded their encouragement, Little One slowly opened the cover.

Immediately a beautiful golden light poured out from the book.

The children stared in wonder as Little One carefully turned the pages and spoke out loud, "This book is about a King...a King who made the whole entire world! He made the trees and oceans...and people...he made everything! And then he gave laws and rules to help people live..."

Clutter pulled a magnifying glass from his pack and nervously leaned forward for a closer look, while Confusion made sure his glasses were in place.

"Do you think this is for real?" asked Little One, "I mean a real King who really made everything?"

"What do you mean is this for real?" Scoffer said, "How could one King possibly make the whole world?"

"Nobody made the world!" Hostility spoke sharply, "You know what they teach us: there was a big explosion one day... and boom! Animals and birds and people everywhere!"

"But not right away," Chaos said anxiously, "It took a long time. First it went 'boom!' and then years and years and years later—that's when the birds and people and stuff showed up."

"Hey, maybe that will work in my room!" Clutter said with nervous excitement, "It looks just like that—boom! And now, if I wait a long, long time, it might just become new and clean and wonderful!"

Little One continued to flip through the Book. "Well, anyway, if this book is true, why didn't anyone ever tell us about it?"

"Because it's *not* true!" said Trouble. "It's just a *book*—just a book with a bunch of stories!"

"Yeah," said Hostility, with her hands on her hips, "and even if it were true, if this King did make everything, then what? If I could meet this King, I have a few things I'd like to say to him!"

"And if there ever was a King, where is he now?" Slander said.

"I'll tell you where he is," Trouble said, pulling away from the Book, his voice getting louder and louder. "He's gone, and he's never coming back! He just took off and left everyone to do what they wanted. He just left! He just left, and he's never coming back! Never! He just left us here to figure things out on our own!" Trouble suddenly realized everyone had gone quiet and they were all staring at him; Little One was very pale.

Clutter, Chaos, and Confusion nodded and said, "And we *can't* figure things out on our own."

The children stood quietly around the Book, watching the soft golden light pour into the room. "Well, one thing is for sure, this Book really is something special," Hostility murmured, touching the glowing pages. Little One watched Hostility and found herself wondering what her friend would look like if she ever smiled. *Pretty,* Little One decided. *She would look really pretty.* Then Little One thought about her other friends. *What would Clutter, Chaos, and Confusion be like if they could just relax? What would happen if Scoffer and Slander started to use nice words? And Trouble. What would it take for him to sing happy, hopeful songs?*

Trouble interrupted the silence. "Well, if there was a King... if there *is* a King," he sneered, "he's forgotten all about us. Let's get out of here."

"Wait!" said Little One, "Maybe the King in this Book hasn't forgotten us! Maybe it's *us* who have forgotten the King! The Land of Laws Forgotten; haven't you ever wondered why this country is called that?"

Clutter, Chaos, and Confusion shook their heads anxiously, "No, I've never wondered. Have you ever wondered? No, I've never wondered. Have you ever wondered? No, I've never wondered."

Everyone stood for a moment, considering what Little One had said; then Trouble spoke out, "Well, if we've forgotten this storybook King, I think it's good! You heard the city leaders singing—we do what's right in our own eyes; that's the way it should be!"

"Yeah!" Scoffer agreed. "Around here we can do what we want! We don't need any laws!"

"We are self-motivated, self-assertive, self-reliant, and self-assured! We have self-awareness, self-esteem, and self-confidence. As a result, we are increasingly self-helped, self-regulated, and self-affirming! We practice self-talk, self-improvement, and self-importance!" Slander finished the list without taking a breath, and when he saw the surprised expressions of his friends, he held up his notebook, "I wrote it down!"

Clutter was still nervously peering at the Book with his magnifying glass. "If there really is a King, I wonder if he knows what's been going on in his world?"

Chaos nodded, biting his fingernails, "He wouldn't like it!"

"Somebody should tell him!" Little One exclaimed. "He ought to know!"

Confusion nodded. "Yeah, then maybe he would come back and fix everything."

"Hey, how come this book was hidden, anyway? Somebody put it underneath all this stuff in a dusty attic; why would they do that?" asked Little One. Then she looked at Trouble, "Do you think this Book might be the reason they don't want anyone coming here?"

"It's a book, Little One!" Trouble almost yelled. "Yeah, sure... it's a special book, but it's just a book! It's a bunch of made-up stories!"

For the first time since she could remember, Little One stepped away from Trouble and said, "I'm going to look for him! I'm going to look for the King!"

Her friends were amazed. "What! How will you ever find him? You don't even know if he exists!"

Little One squared her shoulders purposefully. "I'm going to the Big Hill," she said. "I'll be back in a while."

Clutter looked at her through the magnifying glass and nodded. "We'll stay here and see what else we can find out!"

"Oh, whatever," said Trouble. "Go ahead and try, but it won't do any good. If there ever was a King, he's gone and he's never coming back. I'm going to have a nap."

Little One sneaked out of the attic, unnoticed by Opposition and the others in Government Hall, but *not* unnoticed by three dark creatures lurking in the shadows, nervously picking their noses.

"They're just kids," Corruption whispered, and Pride agreed, "They are insignificant! Them finding the Book means nothing, absolutely nothing!"

But Greed shook his head, remembering another group of children. "I wouldn't be so sure," he said, his voice trembling in fear, "I wouldn't be so sure."

Little One tiptoed out from Government Hall, crept through the dreary streets of the city, and headed toward the Big Hill at the edge of Laws Forgotten. She had never been to the hill before, but she had heard that sometimes people went there to be alone and think, especially if they needed to make a big decision. As she climbed the slope, Little One grew uncertain. It suddenly seemed quite foolish to look for a King she had read about in a book. Like Trouble said, it was just a book. Maybe there was a King...but maybe there wasn't. And if there was a King, how could she expect him to hear her? And if by some miracle he did hear, why would he pay any attention to an orphan kid called "Little One?" She sighed, but kept climbing.

She reached the top of the hill and stood there, wondering what to do. Then she thought again about her friends: Hostility's bruises, Trouble's dark moods, Clutter, Chaos, and Confusion's constant nervous worrying, and she decided it was worth a try.

Little One took a deep breath, squared her shoulders, and called out...timidly at first, then with growing determination. "King? King! Hey, King—are you out there somewhere? I have to talk to you! It's important! KING! King...?"

I need to know...really need to know—
If you are really there.
I need to know...really need to know—If you care.
I'm just a little one—not important but
If you can hear me, please answer
The children here really need
Who you seem to be
'Cause we live in Laws Forgotten
I need to know...really know—If you are really there.
I need to know...really know—If you care..."

Her voice sank to a whisper. "King," she said, "All the kids in Laws Forgotten—Trouble, Hostility, Scoffer, Slander, Clutter, Chaos, Confusion, and the rest—we all need to know if you are real. Life here is like some messed-up game, and no one knows what the rules are. Everyone is doing what they want and cheating and making up new rules that suit them. King...are you real? Did you make this world? Do you care what is happening to it? Do you care what is happening to *us?* King, please answer me! Please!"

At that very moment, Seeker and his friends watched in amazement as the King motioned for Compassion to stand close to him. The King placed his hand over hers and then, with Compassion, the King reached right through the Window of the Secret Place toward Little One. A soft wind reached Little One and she breathed in sudden surprise. Sinking to her knees, she wrapped her arms around her chest and closed her eyes. A flood of tears poured down her cheeks and she smiled. Little One knelt like that for long moments, then stood up, wiped her tears, and headed back down the hill toward Laws Forgotten.

"Wow," said NewName, impressed. "King, you sure know how to communicate!"

"Did you hear what she said," Giggles asked with laughter in her voice, "She *really* wants to know!"

"And now she knows, right King?" asked KnowSo.

"She felt my touch," the King nodded. "She is *beginning* to know."

"King!" Seeker said excitedly, "We'll go and tell Little One and the other kids about you! Then we'll bring them back here to the Kingdom!" The other children agreed enthusiastically, but to their great surprise, the King shook his head.

"No," he said firmly, "Not this time. I want you to take the Kingdom to them!"

"Take the Kingdom to them?" the children wondered.

Doodle and Do spoke together. "We couldn't *do* that!"

Giggles took hold of the King's hand and gently tried to explain, "King, we're not big enough to lift the castle."

The King put back his head and laughed. "You don't have to lift the castle!" he said, "The castle is inside of you! My Kingdom is in your hearts; it shines from your eyes, and it shows through the actions of your life!"

The children peered down at themselves in wonder. "Whoa...I didn't know that! Did you know that?"

KnowSo shook his head. "No, I didn't know that."

"You're amazing, King," Giggles said, still holding his hand.

"I want you to go to Little One and her friends. I want you to be messengers for me, and I want my Kingdom to come to them—right where they are!" the King announced. "I want you to carry my Kingdom!"

The children stood quietly looking up at the King, trying to make sense of what he had told them. The King laughed again at their expressions and then opened the Great Book. "Look here," he said, pointing at a page and reading out loud, "I want my Kingdom to be everywhere; I want it to cover the whole earth! The Kingdom isn't always something you can see with your eyes because the Kingdom is within you."

Giggles laughed with understanding. "We are carriers of the Kingdom!"

"We'll *do* our best to carry your Kingdom, King," said Doodle.

The King smiled at the earnest young faces surrounding him. "I am always with you, even though you might not see me. Now, go!"

"Yes, Sir," Seeker and his friends saluted and then hurried out from the Secret Place toward the Land of Laws Forgotten.

Chapter Four

When Little One returned to the attic, some of the children were still gathered around the Great Book, and others got up from their naps with big yawns. "Little One! You're back!" Clutter, Chaos, and Confusion greeted her.

Scoffer and Slander mocked, "So...did you find the *King?* What did he look like, huh?"

"Did you tell him I want to talk to him?" Hostility sneered, with a big stretch.

"Well, I called..." Little One responded, "...but no one answered..."

"I knew it!" Trouble yawned. "The book is just a bunch of stories. Well anyway, I sure had a great nap!"

"C'mon!" growled Hostility, "Let's get out of here!"

Little One stood in their way. "Wait! Let me finish what I was going to say! The King didn't answer, but I'm very sure that he heard me! I felt..."

"Shh!" Trouble put a finger to his lips, "What was that?"

Everyone froze, listening intently. Sure enough, there was a noise outside the door! Had they been discovered? There was no place to hide! Hostility panicked, pulling at her sleeves anxiously— was it her parents? Why had she followed Trouble? Suddenly there was a knock at the door. The children held their breath and braced themselves for what might happen as the attic door slowly opened... and a boy they had never seen before came into the room.

"Hi," he said, "My name is Seeker, and these are some of my friends..." Compassion and the kids from the Kingdom entered the attic, and the children of Laws Forgotten stood in silent amazement as a golden light entered the room as well; a light just like the one from the Book.

Seeker walked toward Little One. "You were out on the Hill awhile ago, right?"

"Yeah...?" Little One answered cautiously.

"Well, the King sent us here with a message for you...for all of you."

"The King sent you?" exclaimed Little One. "See? I told you that he heard me!"

"Oh yeah?" said Trouble and Hostility together, "What's the message?"

Seeker responded quietly. "The King wants you to know that the Great Book is much more than 'just a bunch of stories' and he didn't go away and 'just leave you to figure things out on your own!'"

Trouble gasped. The King had heard what he said!

"You live in the Land of Laws Forgotten," Seeker continued, "but the King has not forgotten you! The people here turned their backs on the King and decided to forget him; he has been waiting for someone to *really* want to know the truth."

"And when you kids *really* wanted to *know*, he sent us!" said KnowSo.

"Isn't it exciting?" Giggles giggled.

Scoffer sneered at Giggles and repeated her sarcastically, "Isn't it exciting? No, it's not! And who's that anyway?"

Compassion stepped forward and her eyes were glistening with tears. "My name is Compassion....I used to be called Loneliness, but the King changed my name when he rescued me from my life of darkness. He rescued me, and also my son..."

"Hi, I'm NewName!"

"NewName?" Slander sneered, "What kind of name is that!"

Little One spoke up defensively, "I think it's a nice name!"

Trouble sauntered over, snapping his fingers, "Well *my* name is

Trouble. Let me spell that for you: T-R-O-U-B-L-E. Trouble. It's my name and I like it! I don't need some King changing it for me!"

Clutter, Chaos, and Confusion looked at each other and then Clutter stepped forward nervously, "I've never liked my name very much," he said, "I think I'd really like it if the King gave me a new one."

"Same here!" Chaos and Confusion said together.

Seeker looked around at the children of Laws Forgotten, "The King will do more than just change your names!" he said, "The King will change your whole life. He will make it an adventure!"

"Can we tell you our story?" Compassion asked. Clutter, Chaos, Confusion, Hostility, Trouble, Slander, Scoffer, and Little One had never met someone as beautiful and gentle as Compassion. When they looked at her eyes, it was almost like seeing a castle shining out from inside her.

Trouble hesitated, "Well, I guess there *might* be a King. I mean, how else would these kids know where to find us?"

One by one, they sat on the floor and listened as she and NewName told their very sad...and then very happy story...the story of what the King had done. Compassion sang a song about the King and the words seemed to be wrapped in light.

> *In a world that's filled with problems*
> *We know someone who can solve them*
> *He's the Truth, he's the Life, the Way*
> *In a world that's filled with sorrow*
>
> *He gives hope for tomorrow*
>
> *He's the Truth, he's the Life, the Way!*
> *Peace, peace, peace...the King will give*
> *Peace, peace, peace...the King will give*
> *Peace and righteousness and joy.*

Then Compassion showed the children of Laws Forgotten verses in the Great Book about the Kingdom of Light and about how the King loved them and wanted to be with them forever. Little One watched Trouble, hoping he would believe what Compassion was saying. Every person Trouble had ever loved had left and never come back. Hostility pulled her sleeves down tighter and rubbed her arms when NewName talked about how his life had been filled with anger and abuse. And Slander, Scoffer, Clutter, Chaos, and Confusion didn't know what to think.

When Compassion and NewName finished talking, Seeker said, "There truly is a Kingdom and there truly is a King, and you can get to know Him, if you *really* want to."

Doodle stood beside Seeker, "So, how about it? *Do* you believe that the King is real and that his Book is true?"

The children of Laws Forgotten looked at each other and shrugged. "Well, we *want* to believe it."

"*Do* you want to get to know the King?" asked Do.

"You mean we could?"

"Sure!" Seeker winked at the others, and they all very deliberately folded their arms and shook their heads. "But you must *really* want to know the King! Do you *really* want to?!"

The children of Laws Forgotten hesitated only a moment; then stood up straighter and answered with all their hearts. "*Yes!* We *really* want to!"

"Then you *shall* know the King!"

Suddenly the attic flooded with the brightest light they had ever seen, and Seeker and his friends cried out, "King! You're here! So is your Kingdom! It really happened!"

The King smiled and hugged his friends, but he was looking beyond them at the group of children huddled together beside the Great Book, a group of children scarcely hoping to believe what they were experiencing. Light. Huge, amazing, warm, overpowering, wonderful, golden light! They were shielding their eyes and squinting, trying to see.

"I'm here," said the King, dropping to his knees and reaching out his arms toward them. "Come."

Little One was the first to move, and as she took one step toward the King, she was instantly in his arms. "Welcome to my Kingdom!" said the King, his eyes shining.

"I *knew* you were *really* there...I *knew* you heard me," she said, snuggling into his arms with a happy sigh.

One by one, the children of Laws Forgotten stepped forward. Three little boys, the children of Affluence, stood quietly before the King. The King laughed softly as he touched them, and his voice seemed like a wind that blew their past bewilderment somewhere far, far away. "Clutter, Chaos, and Confusion...no more...I am changing you to Clarity, Sense, and Order. Welcome...to my Kingdom."

The little girl who had been so filled with anger and frustration and pain heard the gentle voice of the King, "Hostility... What is it that you wanted to talk to me about?"

Hostility was shocked. The King had heard her say that! She looked at him and suddenly the words just came tumbling out of her mouth, "I'm worried about my parents! They hurt me all the time, and if someone ever found out, maybe they would take me away; and I don't want to go away! I love my mom and dad, and I know they have lots of stress and problems, but, but I just wish they would be nice to me! I try so hard to be good! I do! I try so hard!" Hostility collapsed in tears, and together the King and Compassion held her close; as she cried it was as if her tears washed away the person she had been, and the King healed the pain and the bruises from the inside out. When her sobs finally subsided, the King whispered, "Your new name is Harmony."

"Thank you, King," she whispered, smiling. "It's a beautiful name."

Then the King turned as Trouble stepped forward hesitantly. "Ah, yes...here comes Trouble...you have spent your life being troubled and disappointed, but now you will learn to trust and believe." The King took him by the shoulders and looked directly into his eyes, "I will never leave you or disappoint you. I won't go away or abandon you. I will be with you always, and forever. I will help you figure things out. In fact, I will give you wisdom and purpose and direction in life."

The other children watched in amazement as the boy suddenly stood taller and a golden light shone from his eyes. The King called NewName to his side. "Would you like to help me? What shall his new name be?"

NewName blushed with pleasure at being asked to help the King. He thought for just a moment, then said confidently, "Troubadour!"

Seeker and his friends turned to KnowSo with puzzled faces. "Troubadour? It sounds good, but what does it mean?"

"I know!" said KnowSo, "A troubadour is someone who travels around telling stories...usually with music!"

The King nodded, "It is a good name. Let's spell it T-R-U-E-badour! I will show you the truth, and you will tell stories about me and my Kingdom. You will sing about truth and hope. From now on, you will only cause trouble for the enemies of my Kingdom! What do you think about that, son?"

"T-R-U-E....True-badour....I like it!" he said, snapping his fingers and beginning to hum. "I like it a lot!" The True-badour's eyes glinted with a new, happy kind of mischief, "I'm with you, King!"

The King leaned forward and winked, "And I...am with you!" he laughed.

Everyone laughed together for a few minutes and then realized that two children were still in the darkness. True-badour turned and called to Slander and Scoffer, "Hey guys, come on and meet the King!"

Slander and Scoffer had been trying to shield their eyes from the Light. The brightness terrified them; it made them see the truth about themselves, and they hated that feeling. They heard the other children talking, but they couldn't see who they were talking to. When True-badour called to them, Slander and Scoffer couldn't stand the brightness any longer. "No!" they cried together. "This is weird! This is fake! You are all out of your minds!" And they bolted for the attic door.

Little One tried to stop them, but they pushed her to the floor, "Get away weirdo!" they shouted.

Little One sat on the floor, shocked and hurt, and called out, "But we're friends! Wait!" Then she turned to the King, "Will you go after them? Will you *make* them come back?"

The King sadly shook his head, and Compassion bent to wrap her arms around Little One. NewName stood watching intently, considering, and then said, "King, isn't there a verse in the Great Book about Little One?"

The King nodded. "Yes. My Book says that a little one shall lead." The King studied Little One thoughtfully and then continued, "I won't change your name. Instead, I will change the way that people look at you. There are some *big* adventures ahead for you, Little One!"

The King pulled her to her feet and looked slowly at each young face. "I will use all of you to lead the way for many, many people to enter my Kingdom. Some will choose not to follow my ways, like Scoffer and Slander, but it will not be because they didn't have the opportunity. Yes...the little ones shall lead; the children of Laws Forgotten will cause my truth to be remembered! You still live in Laws Forgotten, but you are no longer part of this world!" the King declared. "You have passed from Darkness into Light! From this day forward, my Kingdom is within you! Seeker, NewName, Compassion, and the others will help you learn what it means to be carriers of my Kingdom. Let my light shine in the darkness around you; be strong and filled with courage! I am with you!"

And as suddenly as he had appeared, the King was gone. Harmony, Clarity, Sense, and Order, True-badour and Little One looked around, amazed, "Where did he go?"

"He's still here," Seeker explained, "Even though you can't see him!"

"Now that you belong to him, the King is always, always with you," Compassion assured them. "And his Kingdom is inside of you!"

"*Inside* of us!"

Compassion nodded. "You are now carriers of the Kingdom! Come on everyone, let's show these kids what the Great Book has to say about that!"

And outside the attic door, three very frightened dragons were shaking so much they could hardly pick their noses.

Chapter Five

The children of Laws Forgotten met every day in the attic to study the Great Book. Compassion, Seeker, and the other Kingdom kids often joined them, and together they spent hours learning more about the King and his Kingdom. The light that had filled the attic now filled the children of Laws Forgotten! And the more they studied the Great Book, the more the light began to shine out from inside of them. Time passed. And as time passed, they became more and more like their new names.

True-badour developed his musical talent. He sang words from the Great Book, and his songs were like musical stories that the other children loved to listen to. Sometimes Harmony would sing along, and her friends were constantly amazed at how pretty she looked when she smiled. Clarity, Sense, and Order were calm and peaceful; and now that they weren't confused and worried about everything, they were learning how to laugh and have fun.

People noticed the changes in the children—at home, at school, and throughout the city people began to talk.

They've been changed! They've been re-arranged!
They've been changed! They are not the same
There's something happening deep inside of them
It shows up in their words and actions and—
I don't know what's happened—but they've changed!

The day arrived when the Land of Laws Forgotten would rename the Ruling Opposition as their leader, and that morning

Hugh Manism and M.T. Entertainment went to speak with Strife, Opposition, and Affluence.

"We must talk to you about your children," M.T. Entertainment began. "The sign for my theatre finally arrived the other day, and no sooner had I hung it up, than those kids came in and asked me to take it down! They claimed it was *inappropriate!* What right do they have to tell me that? They know very well that around here everyone does what is right in their own eyes!"

He paused uncomfortably for a moment, then continued, "Their eyes. That's what got me, actually. It was the strangest thing. Every time I looked at those kids, I was sure I saw a...a castle in their eyes!"

"Castle?" echoed Strife.

"That's right! They keep referring to some King and his invisible Kingdom. Whoever heard of such things?"

"I have been hearing about it far too much!" declared M.T. Entertainment. Then he spoke directly to Strife and her husband, his tone suspicious, "That daughter of yours sure has changed, hasn't she? I've never seen such sweetness from anyone in your family! What are you up to, Opposition? Trying to get your kid to win votes for you?"

Opposition sputtered, struggling to find words to respond, when Hugh Manism spoke up, "The children have all been displaying abnormal behavior. I am deeply concerned that they must remain free-thinking and as a law unto themselves! Take for instance that rascal, Trouble; he has been talking about what he refers to as 'absolute truth!'"

The others responded with horrified gasps and Hugh Manism continued, *"Now* do you understand the urgency of the new text book, 'Everyone's Rules Are Right?' The children all go on and on about a King and about his way being the *only* right way!"

Affluence cleared her throat. She had been unusually quiet

throughout the discussion, but now she said, "I have also noticed significant changes in the children; and I, too, have seen a light in their eyes. It reminds me of a Kingdom I heard about once...."

"What!" the others exclaimed.

Affluence nodded. "Clutter, Chaos, and Confusion offered to help me organize the shelves in one of the stores the other day. I know that comes as quite a shock, I myself was very surprised...and when they were working, it was like they were actually happy to be helping me! And I saw it...a light in all of their eyes...it was bright and shining and...."

"Rubbish!" exclaimed Strife. "This kind of talk must stop! It's nothing but brain-washing!"

"Perhaps they might need their brains washed a bit?" Affluence asked hesitantly. "I know my boys..."

"Your boys are just fine!" Strife declared. "They are a lively bunch, certainly, but that just shows they are self-motivated!"

"Self-motivated!" Hugh Manism spoke up. "And that is a quality that is certainly valued here in Laws Forgotten! We work very hard to teach the children to be self-motivated, self-assertive, self-reliant, and self-assured!"

Affluence shook her head as if coming out of a daze and interrupted, "You're right! What was I thinking? Of course they don't need their heads filled with nonsense about some higher law!" She repeated the last phrase with a threatening look at Opposition, "Higher *law!* Something must be done about the kids!"

Strife stood more closely to her husband and announced, "Good citizens of Laws Forgotten, please *remember* that you have a wonderful leader who will be sure to look after this *little* problem!" She poked Opposition sharply in the ribs, "Won't you *dear?*"

"Who? Me!" Opposition responded with a combination of false modesty and fear.

The city leaders leaned toward him and added menacingly, "Find out why the children have changed; find out who is brain-washing them and put a stop to it! Or else!"

As the leaders marched away, Strife spoke to her husband. "Today is the day when you are to be renamed as the Ruling Opposition of Laws Forgotten, or don't you *remember?*" Her voice lowered threateningly, and Strife continued. "But this could wreck everything! All that we have worked for—our own rights, our own way of doing things! Find out what is happening to the children! And put a stop to it!"

She turned abruptly, leaving Opposition standing, wiping his brow, and wringing his hands under the pressure. And then...from the shadows of Laws Forgotten, some nasty, smelly dragons moved toward Opposition, picking their noses in a most disgusting manner...

Chapter Six

"**I**t's all up to you..." Pride said softly. "You have to do something..."

Although Opposition could not see the dragons, their words echoed through his mind. "It's all up to me...I have to do something..."

"Public opinion is turning against you..." Corruption whispered.

"Public opinion is turning against me..."

"You have to hang on to your position..." Greed continued.

"I have to hang on to my position..."

Pride put an invisible arm around Opposition's shoulder. "You have to stop the kids, or everything you have built will be lost..."

Opposition shuddered. "I have to stop the kids, or everything I have built will be lost..."

"Stop the kids! Stop the kids!" the dragons taunted.

"Stop the kids! Stop the kids!" Opposition echoed, deep in thought. "But how?"

The dragons were deep in thought as well. "Hmmm," mused Corruption, "I'm thinking about the other two children— Scoffer and Slander. They clearly made the choice to remain on our side...."

Pride's eyes flashed, "Ah, yes...they chose to turn away from the Light when it was offered, and they chose to stay in Darkness..."

"Perhaps Scoffer and Slander should join forces with Greed and Corruption!" Pride snickered, "Why don't you go and find them and I'll stay right here." And so Greed and Corruption went to find Scoffer and Slander, while Pride stayed with Opposition repeating, "Stop the kids! Stop the kids!"

Just then, the children of Laws Forgotten came down the street, laughing happily. Opposition quickly drew back and hid from their view.

Little One was in the lead. "This is so great! Everyone in town is wondering about the changes they've seen in us!"

"It's just like the King said," True-badour added, "we're bringing his Light into the Darkness!"

"All because of the Book!" declared Harmony.

Opposition listened from his hiding place and trembled. "Book...what book? They couldn't have found *the* book..."

Pride stood nearby and whispered in his ears, and Opposition stopped trembling and began to pick his nose like the dragon, in a most disgusting manner. Opposition laughed a very evil laugh as he stepped through a doorway behind him. "Well now, my little Kingdom believers, you are about to meet with...Opposition."

The children, unaware that Pride and Opposition had over-heard them, continued their conversation. "There's going to be a big celebration in Government Hall Park today," Clarity announced. "I think the time is right!"

True-badour nodded. "The time is right for this place to become the Land of Laws Remembered!"

Harmony smiled. "What's the plan, True-badour? We're with you!"

"And I—am with you!" True-badour laughed. "Clarity, Sense, and Order, you and Harmony go on ahead; Little One and I will go and get the Book!"

True-badour smiled at Little One's enthusiasm as they walked toward Government Hall. "Slow down a bit!" he said, "A lot of people will be around today. We need to be nice and quiet!"

Little One stopped and held her hand over her heart solemnly, "Nice and quiet!"

They both laughed, remembering back to the first time they had snuck up the attic stairs. "So much has happened to us since that day we found the Great Book!" said Little One. "Because of that Book, our lives have changed!"

"And, now," True-badour nodded, "because of that Book, many more lives will *be* changed!"

They laughed excitedly and continued through the city streets. When Little One and True-badour reached Government Hall, they were relieved to see the heavy door was open for all the visitors to enter. They carefully watched for an opportunity to sneak unnoticed up into the balcony and through the attic door. Together, they lifted the Great Book out from the drawer. True-badour held it close, and they were just heading toward the door when True-badour put a finger to his lips.

"Shh! What was that?"

Little One froze, listening intently. Sure enough, there was a noise! Had they been discovered? There was no place to hide! The children held their breath and braced themselves for what might happen. And then...Opposition stepped out from the shadows, holding his cane to block the doorway.

"What do you think you are doing?" He growled, his voice dark and raspy and evil.

The children trembled in fear for just a moment; then courage took their hearts. Little One stood as tall as she could and proclaimed, "We are taking the Great Book to Government Hall Park!"

Opposition spoke slowly and deliberately. "But that Book is not yours; it doesn't belong to you."

True-badour stepped in front of Little One. "Yes it does! It belongs to everyone! And we're going to take it to the people of Laws Forgotten—so they can remember!"

"But some things are best forgotten," answered Opposition, pretending to be gentle. "You children are too young for all this. Give me the Book, and we'll just forget anything ever happened."

True-badour hung on tightly to the Great Book. "No! It's not time to forget; it's time to remember! And this Book belongs to us! It belongs to everyone!"

"But somebody put it away in a dusty attic," Little One said quietly. "I wonder why they would do that? Why would somebody want to hide the truth?"

True-badour looked at Opposition, "Is this Book the reason you don't want anyone coming here?"

Opposition spoke, pretending to be gentle. "You children are too young for all this. Give me the Book, and we'll just forget anything ever happened. Give it to me...*now.*" His voice suddenly turned hard, and Opposition stepped toward True-badour and Little One.

Clarity, Sense, Order, and Harmony stood waiting anxiously in Government Hall Park.

"Something is wrong," Order whispered. "True-badour and Little One should have been here by now!"

"Do you feel it?" Sense asked. "There's something evil and nasty going on around here!"

Clarity shivered, "Yes! I feel it!"

"Let's call to the King!" Harmony said, urging them into a little huddle. "We'll make a Secret Place right here!"

In the attic, True-badour looked past Opposition and pointed. "Look, Little One. This is not about Opposition; at least not *this* opposition."

Little One gasped, "A dragon! The Great Book talks about dragons, the rulers of Darkness...so, that's who is behind all of this! Of course!"

"Dragon?" muttered Opposition. "What dragon? I don't see any dragon."

"Ha!" True-badour exclaimed, handing the Great Book to Little One and rolling up his sleeves. "Well, look out, dragon, here comes trouble!"

"Why did you do it, Opposition?" Little One asked, "Why did you hide the Great Book? Why did you take the King's laws away from the people?"

Pride swelled to become a huge shadow. He threw words into Opposition's mind and the man screamed, "I will be supreme ruler! I will be king! I will climb up and set my throne as high as the clouds! I will be king of the whole world!"

"There is only one King!" declared True-badour. "He is the true King, the Creator of everything, and he *opposes* you and your pride!"

Little One held up the Great Book and called out, "King! Help! Help!!!"

Light filled the attic. Huge, amazing, warm, overpowering, wonderful, golden light! Opposition shielded his eyes, and Pride screamed in absolute terror and rage, furiously struggling against unseen chains.

The King calmly took the Great Book from Little One, opened it and read directly to Opposition, "You have rebelled and denied the true King. I know how unfair and oppressive you have been, carefully planning deceitful lies. Your government courts oppose the righteous, and *justice* is nowhere to be found. Truth stumbles in the streets, honesty has been outlawed, and anyone who renounces evil is attacked."

The King calmly turned the pages and read more, this time speaking directly to the dragon Pride, who was still furiously struggling against unseen chains. "You said, 'I will be supreme ruler! I will be king! I will climb up and set my throne as high as the clouds! I will be king of the whole world.' But instead, you will be brought down to the underground pit, down to its lowest depths!"

The King turned the pages again and motioned for Little One to read, "We use the King's mighty weapons to knock down the strongholds of human reasoning and to destroy false arguments. We destroy every proud obstacle that keeps people from knowing the King." And then the King showed her where to read from one of the final pages in the Book, "And the great dragon, the ancient serpent, the one deceiving the whole world, will be thrown down and defeated!"

Pride cowered and screamed in pain and rage as the King handed the Great Book to True-badour, "Go ahead!" said the King, "Cause some trouble!"

True-badour laughed, took hold of the Great Book, and stretched it out toward Pride. "Dragon! You have controlled this land for too long! Now, in the name of the King, get out of here!" With an anguished cry, Pride shriveled back into the shadows and disappeared.

And then True-badour and the King sang a song that made the attic and the entire Government Hall and Government Hall Park absolutely rock! (Clarity, Sense, and Order and Harmony looked up from their Secret Place huddle and smiled with relief.)

Here comes trouble...
Get lookin' out dragons—we're comin' for you!
Here comes trouble
We're fighting for right, and we're
bringing back truth
Here comes trouble....

We're gonna cause some really big trouble
For dragons that are hangin' around
We're gonna cause some really big trouble
And we're gonna bring them....down....!
T-R-O-U-B-L-E

That spells trouble for the enemy
T-R-O-U-B-L-E
I'm with the King and the King is with me
Here comes trouble....

As the song finished, the King swung Little One around in the air, winked at True-badour, and disappeared. Opposition stood rubbing his eyes, swaying weakly, and looking confused.

"What?" he mumbled. "Where am I? Who are you? What are you doing?"

Little One helped him stand. "It's us, the kids...we came to get the Great Book!"

"That's right!" said True-badour, "and we're taking the Great Book to the celebration in Government Hall Park!"

Opposition stared at them blankly, "What? Oh, by all means! Of course! Yes, that's a fine idea! Take the Great Book to Government Hall Park! Just as...just as I should have done...a long time ago...." Opposition continued to ramble on as True-badour and Little One looked at each other with smiles of wonder and took him by the arm. "Yes, yes," Opposition continued, "That is a fine idea! Just as...just as I should have done a long time ago! Yes, yes, by all means! Take the Great Book to Government Hall Park!"

Chapter Seven

Government Hall Park was decorated with mismatched bright flags and streamers. Rude and tattered minstrels were playing and great tables of candy-coated food were set out for the crowd of townspeople and city leaders that had gathered, awaiting the Ruling Opposition's appearance. How very surprised they all were when Opposition arrived, surrounded by a group of children!

And how much more surprised they were when Opposition escorted Little One to the platform! A gasp went through the crowd as True-badour lifted the Great Book onto the podium, and the people watched in breathless silence when Little One opened the cover and began to read.

As Little One read words from the Great Book, True-badour sang softly about the Light and the Kingdom, and a miracle happened in the Land of Laws Forgotten. Opposition hugged his wife, and she blew her nose loudly; Affluence knelt and wept as her sons put their arms around her shoulders; and Hugh Manism, M.T. Entertainment, and the other city leaders shook their heads in a daze, trying to remember...

Little One closed the Book, lifted her eyes, and said, "Oh, King, you made the heavens and the earth. You didn't just go off and leave us. We went off and left you! Please forgive us. Please forgive all the children and the mothers and fathers and all the people who have been leading our country. Oh, King, we need you! We need your Kingdom to come..."

But then, just as Light was about to come to the Land of Laws Forgotten, the atmosphere suddenly darkened and trembled with a feeling of intense evil.

Slander and Scoffer pushed their way through the crowd, and the people backed away, terrified. These were no longer the children who had walked the streets the day before; they seemed to have grown older and stronger and nastier. The dragons Greed and Corruption walked unseen beside Slander and Scoffer, spewing slimy nasty thoughts throughout the crowd.

"So, if it isn't the little Kingdom kids!" Scoffer sneered to True-badour and Little One as they approached the podium, "How's the fairytale going, huh?"

"Yeah," Slander joined in. "Fairytales...getting everyone in Laws Forgotten to notice you, huh! And trying to get them all to believe like you do, huh?"

"Just who do you think you are, anyway—showing off and going around town being all helpful and 'shining the light!' It's all about making us look bad, isn't it? Are you saying you are better than us? Huh?" Scoffer accused. "Well, the fairytale is over!"

Slander turned and spoke to the crowd, who had been watching and not knowing how to respond. "Citizens and leaders of Laws Forgotten! These children are trespassers and liars!"

"And thieves!" Scoffer shouted.

"What?" True-badour and Little One spoke together, "That's not true!"

"Did you really think you would get away with it?" Slander stood with his arms folded.

"What do you mean by that?" True-badour asked.

"Don't act so innocent!" Scoffer sneered.

Slander pulled out his notebook and pointed to it as he shouted to the crowd, "It's all in here! I've been writing it down and keeping track for months! This group of liars have been hiding out in the attic of Government Hall! And that is trespassing!"

A murmur swept through the crowd, "Trespassing! Attic! Government Hall!"

"Government Hall is open to everyone!" Little One said bravely.

"It is?" mocked Slander. "But didn't Trouble himself tell you that no kids are allowed?"

True-badour's face turned red, and he stammered, "I just said that to make it sound more exciting that day, I didn't mean to...."

"You didn't mean to what?" Scoffer interrupted. "You didn't mean to *lie?* And I thought Kingdom kids always told the truth!"

"You know very well that he said that *before* he got to know the King!" Harmony stepped in.

"I don't care when he said it...he still told a lie!" Scoffer announced.

Another murmur swept through the crowd, "Lies! Trespassing! Attic! Government Hall!"

"You are liars and trespassers and...you are thieves!" Slander shouted and pointed to the Book, "Where did you get that Book!"

"From the attic of Government Hall," True-badour said softly.

"Thieves!" Slander screamed.

"Thieves! Lies! Trespassing! Attic! Government Hall!" The crowd's murmur turned to a loud chant.

"This is the King's Book, and it belongs to everyone!" Little One shouted above the noise. "The King wants us to remember! He wants us to remember, not just his laws, but his love and his justice!"

"Justice!" Opposition had been standing to the side in a daze, but when he heard that word, he came to himself. "Justice! Justice!" he cried. "That is my name! Well, at least, it used to be my name!"

Opposition approached the podium, and True-badour and Little One looked at each other once again with smiles of wonder and took him by the arm, helping him up the step. "Yes, yes," Opposition continued, lifting his voice for all to hear, "Justice! Just as...I should have done a long time ago! Yes, the Great Book must be here at Government Hall Park! The children have done well to bring it here!"

He turned and spoke to Scoffer and Slander, "The Great Book is for all the people, and no slanderers or scoffers or dragons will prevent that from happening. I am Opposition, and I oppose *you!* Now, away with all of you!"

There was true authority in Opposition's voice, and immediately Slander, Scoffer, Greed, Pride, and Corruption turned and ran.

A ripple went through the crowd as they sensed evil departing, and then they looked around, wondering what to do next. Some rubbed their eyes, as if they were just waking up from a dream. Opposition lifted his voice again, "The Great Book has been returned, and now it is time for *us* to turn...our hearts and our lives to the King!"

"To the King!" shouted the crowd, some more loudly than others.

"We are very sorry for having forgotten the King and his laws," Opposition said to the children, the people nodding and encouraging him. "And we want to...we *need to*...get to know the King!"

Little One winked at the others, and they all very deliberately folded their arms and shook their heads. "Do you *really* want to know the King!"

The people hesitated only a moment, then smiled and answered with all their hearts. "YES! We *REALLY* want to!"

"Then you SHALL know the King!" Suddenly, Government Hall Park was flooded with golden light and the children cried out, "King! You're here! So is your Kingdom! It really happened! And hey! Compassion, Seeker, and the others are here, too!"

There was a lot of hugging and greeting each other. The King smiled and held his friends, but he was looking beyond them at the group of people huddled together beside the Great Book, a group of people scarcely hoping to believe what they were experiencing. Light. Huge, amazing, warm, overpowering, wonderful, golden light! They were shielding their eyes and squinting, trying to see.

"I'm here," said the King, reaching out his arms toward them. "Come."

Ruling Opposition was the first to move, and as he took one step toward the King, he was instantly in his arms. "Welcome back to my Kingdom, Justice!" said the King, his eyes shining.

One by one, the people of Laws Forgotten made their decisions. Most stepped toward the King, but a few retreated into the darkness. Little One watched sadly with Compassion when that happened, and she realized the King watched sadly as well. Then Hugh Manism, Affluence, Strife, and M.T. Entertainment stood quietly before the King, looking embarrassed and hopeful at the same time. Pride, Greed, and Corruption had lost their power, and now it was time for a new life and new names.

The King spoke to each one, and his voice seemed like a wind that blew their past mistakes and wrong thinking somewhere far, far away.

"Hugh Manism," the King said, calling the man to stand before him, "I must tell you that everyone's ways are *not* right; and that things like self-help are really no help at all. Self-*denial* and self-*sacrifice* are the kinds of words used in my Kingdom. Are you willing to give up your own ways and your own rights to serve me and what I call *right?*"

"I am willing, your majesty!"

"Are you willing to spend the rest of your life concerned with the needs of others and not the needs of yourself?"

"I am willing, your majesty!"

The King looked at Compassion, who placed her hands on the shoulders of the Director of Schools, and the King spoke, "This day I change your name to Humanity. I put my love for people into your very being, and I give you my power to bring change in the earth!"

The King's words and the touch of Compassion had a powerful effect. Humanity bent low and wept out loud with great tears. The sound of his weeping broke any remaining hardness in the hearts of Strife and Affluence. Compassion moved to touch them as well, and they fell at the King's feet.

Affluence was surrounded by Clarity, Sense, and Order, and she begged, "Great King! I too want to bring change to the earth! I want to use my wealth to help the needy and hungry in the land! I will give to the poor! I will share what I have!"

The King laughed a deep, happy laugh, "Today is the day of salvation! Affluence...I am changing you to True Success!"

And now, M.T. Entertainment....Hmm.

M.T. Entertainment stepped forward, stuttering, "Your Majesty...I...I see now the true nature of my name, and I must say I find it very awkward to stand in front of you...Oh! Of course, I must bow in front of you, not stand! The whole M.T. Entertainment Industry must bow before you, King!"

As M.T. Entertainment knelt, the King said, "If the entertainment industry would bow to my Kingdom, then the world would be filled with much laughter and life and wholeness and truth."

"I see that now, Your Majesty," M.T. Entertainment stuttered, "My associates and I have all been inappropriate to say the least! We've been many other things as well! Is there any hope of a new name, do you suppose?"

The King turned to NewName and asked, "Well, NewName.... what do you think?"

NewName thought hard for a moment and then replied, "Well, King, entertainment can be a good thing, a very good thing—especially if your castle would shine from it and if it carried your Kingdom! Maybe his name can stay Entertainment, and you just take off the 'M.T.' part!"

"Hmm...I like that idea!" the King said, turning to Entertainment, "And now you can decide what will be in front of your name—Good Entertainment...Great Entertainment...

Entertainment nodded, "Or perhaps Family Entertainment, Your Majesty. Families need a lot of help these days," he said, as everyone turned toward Justice and his family.

Strife was weeping uncontrollably, stroking her daughter's arms and sobbing, "I'm sorry! I'm so sorry!"

Harmony hugged her mother close, "I forgive you, Mom. It's OK. I forgive you."

The King gently lifted Strife's head and spoke directly to her heart, "All is forgiven," the King proclaimed, "From now on, Harmony is in your house, and you will be known as Peace." Then the King turned to her husband, "and you...will be Justice Restored!"

Justice was shaking with shame and regret. "It's all my fault! I knew what was going on, but I allowed anger and abuse to continue! Please forgive me! Please forgive me!" Harmony forgave her father, and then he bowed before the King, still shaking with shame and regret. "Oh, Great King, everything really is all my fault!" he wailed. "I turned my back on you! I hid the Great Book from the people, and they forgot your laws! I allowed pride, greed, and corruption to take over the country! I am not worthy of your forgiveness, and yet, you have called me Justice Restored! You have restored my life and my family; now I beg you...please, please help me to restore your truth in the land!"

"All is forgiven," the King declared, "and I *will* help you." Then, his voice lowered and the King spoke words to Harmony, Peace, and Justice that were meant only for them, and the crowd waited patiently. Finally, the family stood up, bowed to the King and looked around with light shining from their eyes. Then Justice Restored walked to the podium, picked up the Great Book, and called the children forward.

"This day we are thankful to Little One," he said. "We are thankful and very grateful to all of our children...for helping us to remember. This day, we declare the Great Book as the guiding book for our lives. This day we declare the Great King as the one and only true King. May his Kingdom come, and his will and purposes be accomplished! May we carry the Light of his Kingdom forever. This day, we declare our country to be the Land of Laws Remembered, Laws Honored, and Laws Lived By!"

"Hooray! Hooray!" the crowd shouted.

"Look!" cried Little One, holding the King's hand and pointing. Government Hall Park was now filled with huge golden Light. The decorations had become royal and beautiful, Truebadour was leading the minstrels in songs of the Kingdom, and the tables were filled with indescribably fresh, tasty, and life-giving foods.

"The King's banquet!" Seeker and his friends shouted. "C'mon!"

The King called everyone to join the celebration, and what a celebration it was! The songs and laughter of that day echoed throughout the city, and Light rushed forward, utterly consuming the Land of Darkness.

A Song from that Celebration

Let your Kingdom come
Let your will be done
In us, and through us today
Let your Kingdom come
Let your will be done
As we lift up our voices in praise.
We are carriers of the Kingdom
Messengers of his love
People will see the King of kings
As they see him in us.
So...let your Kingdom come, we pray.

Think About the Story

When nations put God's laws away and decide to do what they want, the result is clutter, chaos, confusion, hostility, and trouble! We need to pray for the leaders of our cities and countries to remember God's laws and to crown Him as their King and Ruler. The Great Book says in Habakkuk 2:14 that one day the whole earth will be filled with an understanding and knowledge of how wonderful God is. Philippians 2:10-11 tells us that one day every person will bow their knee and acknowledge that Jesus is Lord and King.

Talk to the King

"King Jesus, the Great Book teaches that the Kingdom is within us—we are temples and dwelling places for Your Spirit. WOW! Please help me do a great job of carrying Your Kingdom everywhere I go, every day that I'm alive on this earth—let Your Kingdom come... let Your light shine bright in, and through, ME!"

Read from the King's Book—Isaiah 9:2

The people who walked in darkness
Have seen a great light!
Those who lived in the dragon's land,
On them the light has shined!
(Great Book Paraphrase)

- **Luke 17:21—The Kingdom is within you!**

- **1 Corinthians 3:16; 6:19; 1 Peter 2:5—you are a temple for God to live in!**

- **2 Corinthians 4:6-10—you have this treasure inside your "earthen vessel."**

To Learn More

Visit www.dianlayton.com to discover the SEEKER music CDs, teaching materials, and musical theatre scripts.

Books

Rescued From the Dragon

Secret of the Blue Pouchs

In Search of Wanderer

The Dreamer

Armor of Light

Songs

Secret of the Blue Pouch—The Songs
COVENANT AWARD NOMINATION

In Search of Wanderer—The Songs
COVENANT AWARD WINNER—CHILDREN'S ALBUM OF THE YEAR

Seeker's Great Adventure & Rescued From the Dragon—
The Songs
COVENANT AWARD NOMINATION

Armor of Light—The Songs
COVENANT AWARD NOMINATION

Carriers of the Kingdom—The Songs

Additional copies of this book and other
book titles from DESTINY IMAGE are
available at your local bookstore.

Call toll-free: 1-800-722-6774.

Send a request for a catalog to:

Destiny Image® Publishers, Inc.
P.O. Box 310
Shippensburg, PA 17257-0310

*"Speaking to the Purposes of God for This
Generation and for the Generations to Come."*

**For a complete list of our titles,
visit us at www.destinyimage.com.**